Women's Economic Empowerment in the Indian Ocean Region

This volume brings together influential contemporary research and discussion papers to explore the issue of women's economic empowerment in the Indian Ocean rim. Women's economic empowerment has become a central policy concern of many Indian Ocean rim countries, such as Australia, and of the Indian Ocean Rim Association (IORA). This book highlights a range of perspectives on the issue by examining a variety of case studies. Its aim is to provide research that helps develop evidence-based policy-making, to assist in the better implementation of gender responsive policy frameworks and budgets. The book covers themes such as: regional governance approaches to fostering women's economic empowerment; the obstacles to informal trade; gender bias in policy development; and differing roles and purposes for women's education. This volume is essential reading for all those interested in policy affecting development; trade; women's education; professional training and training; governance structures and practices; and gender equality in the Indian Ocean region.

The chapters in this book were originally published as a special issue of the *Journal of the Indian Ocean Region*.

Timothy Doyle is Professor of Politics and International Studies at the University of Adelaide in Australia, where he teaches Global Environmental Politics, International Political Economy and Political Fiction. He is Chair of Politics and International Relations at Keele University in the United Kingdom. Professor Doyle is also Distinguished Research Fellow at the Australia-Asia-Pacific Institute (AAPI), Curtin University, Western Australia.

Adela Alfonsi is Research Fellow at the University of Adelaide, Australia. She is Commissioning Editor of the *Journal of the Indian Ocean Region* (Taylor & Francis).

Women's Economic Empowerment in the Indian Ocean Region

Edited by
Timothy Doyle and Adela Alfonsi

Routledge
Taylor & Francis Group

LONDON AND NEW YORK

First published 2018
by Routledge

2 Park Square, Milton Park, Abingdon, Oxfordshire OX14 4RN
52 Vanderbilt Avenue, New York, NY 10017

Routledge is an imprint of the Taylor & Francis Group, an informa business

First issued in paperback 2020

British Library Cataloguing in Publication Data
A catalogue record for this book is available from the British Library

ISBN 13: 978-0-8153-7911-9 (hbk)
ISBN 13: 978-0-367-59306-3 (pbk)

Typeset in Myriad Pro
by RefineCatch Limited, Bungay, Suffolk

Publisher's Note
The publisher accepts responsibility for any inconsistencies that may have
arisen during the conversion of this book from journal articles to book chapters,
namely the possible inclusion of journal terminology.

Disclaimer
Every effort has been made to contact copyright holders for their permission to
reprint material in this book. The publishers would be grateful to hear from any
copyright holder who is not here acknowledged and will undertake to rectify
any errors or omissions in future editions of this book.

Contents

Citation Information

The chapters in this book were originally published in the *Journal of the Indian Ocean Region*, volume 13, issue 1 (March 2017). When citing this material, please use the original page numbering for each article, as follows:

Chapter 1
Chief Editor Foreword
Timothy Doyle
Journal of the Indian Ocean Region, volume 13, issue 1 (March 2017), pp. 1–3

Chapter 2
The future of women's economic empowerment in the Indian Ocean region: governance challenges and opportunities
Susan Harris Rimmer
Journal of the Indian Ocean Region, volume 13, issue 1 (March 2017), pp. 4–24

Chapter 3
Opportunities and challenges faced by women involved in informal cross-border trade in the city of Mutare during a prolonged economic crisis in Zimbabwe
Caroline Manjokoto and Dick Ranga
Journal of the Indian Ocean Region, volume 13, issue 1 (March 2017), pp. 25–39

Chapter 4
Recognizing Indonesian fisherwomen's roles in fishery resource management: profile, policy, and strategy for economic empowerment
Athiqah Nur Alami and Sandy Nur Ikfal Raharjo
Journal of the Indian Ocean Region, volume 13, issue 1 (March 2017), pp. 40–53

Chapter 5
The 'Barefoot Model' of economic empowerment in rural Rajasthan
Giulia Mariangela Mininni
Journal of the Indian Ocean Region, volume 13, issue 1 (March 2017), pp. 54–75

Chapter 6
Protecting Indonesia's women migrant workers from the grassroots: a story of Paguyuban Seruni
Elisabeth Dewi and Sylvia Yazid
Journal of the Indian Ocean Region, volume 13, issue 1 (March 2017), pp. 76–91

Chapter 7
Sega *as voice-work in the Indian Ocean region*
Rosabelle Boswell
Journal of the Indian Ocean Region, volume 13, issue 1 (March 2017), pp. 92–110

Chapter 8
Women's economic empowerment in the Indian Ocean region through gender equality in work: building a common agenda
Priya Chacko
Journal of the Indian Ocean Region, volume 13, issue 1 (March 2017), pp. 111–118

Chapter 9
Women's empowerment in the global South
Benito Cao
Journal of the Indian Ocean Region, volume 13, issue 1 (March 2017), pp. 119–124

For any permission-related enquiries please visit:
http://www.tandfonline.com/page/help/permissions

Notes on Contributors

Athiqah Nur Alami is Researcher and PhD student at the National University of Singapore.

Adela Alfonsi is Research Fellow at the University of Adelaide, Australia. She is Commissioning Editor of the *Journal of the Indian Ocean Region*.

Rosabelle Boswell is an Anthropologist and Executive Dean of Arts at Nelson Mandela Metropolitan University, South Africa. She is also Honorary Professor of Anthropology at the University of Cape Town, South Africa. Her research focuses on identity and the management of cultural heritage in the islands of the southwest Indian Ocean region.

Benito Cao is Lecturer of Politics at the University of Adelaide, Australia.

Priya Chacko is Lecturer in International Politics in the Department of Politics and International Studies in the School of Social Sciences at the University of Adelaide, Australia.

Elisabeth Dewi is Lecturer in the Department of International Relations, Parahyangan Catholic University, Indonesia. She is Head of the Parahyangan Centre for International Studies and Editor of *International Relations Academic Journal of Parahyangan Centre for International Studies*.

Timothy Doyle is Professor of Politics and International Studies at the University of Adelaide, Australia, where he teaches Global Environmental Politics, International Political Economy and Political Fiction. He is Chair of Politics and International Relations at Keele University, United Kingdom. He is also Distinguished Research Fellow at the Australia-Asia-Pacific Institute (AAPI), Curtin University, Western Australia.

Susan Harris Rimmer is Australian Research Council Future Fellow in the Asia-Pacific College of Diplomacy at the Australian National University. She is also a Research Associate at the Development Policy Centre in the Crawford School and Associate Professor at Griffith Law School, Australia. She is an expert in women's rights and international law, and has a track record in influencing government to adopt progressive policy ideas.

Caroline Manjokoto is based at the Manicaland Regional Campus at Zimbabwe Open University and has a research interest in development studies and women's empowerment.

Giulia Mariangela Mininni is a PhD student in Environmental Politics at Keele University, UK. Her research draws on concepts of gender inequality and sustainability in order to understand the local impacts of the lack of energy services on women and the implications of this lack for development projects.

Sandy Nur Ikfal Raharjo is Researcher at the Center for Political Research at the Indonesian Institute of Sciences, Indonesia.

Dick Ranga is Senior Lecturer at Zimbabwe Open University. He is an international development expert with experience in researching, lecturing and applying knowledge on the impact of population, migration, gender, poverty and inequality on development.

Sylvia Yazid is Lecturer at the Department of International Relations, Parahyangan Catholic University, Indonesia. Besides teaching and conducting research and community service, she is presently serving as Head of the Department of International Relations.

Foreword

Timothy Doyle

Women's Economic Empowerment is a central project of the Indian Ocean Rim Association (IORA). At least two international conferences on this topic have already been held under IORA's auspices. At the 2013 IORA Council of Ministers' Meeting (COMM), women's economic empowerment was identified as a cross-cutting theme which would be integrated across all 6 of IORA's priority areas. Building on this, along with the United Nations Development Program, Australia co-hosted the 'Women's Economic Empowerment with a Focus on Tourism and Textiles in the IORA Countries' conference in Kuala Lumpur in August 2014 (IORA, 2014). The conference examined the challenges and opportunities for women's entrepreneurship, the role of civil society in supporting women's economic empowerment, and promoting trade reforms. Participants included all member states of IORA, as well as academics and business. In its summary report prepared the Australian Department of Foreign Affairs and Trade (DFAT, 2014), produced six priority messages for supporting women's economic empowerment in the IOR, as follows:

1. Invest in women's education, professional development and training
2. Promote national cultural identity – self, product and place – in a way that encompasses the strengths and contribution of women
3. Contribute to broader understanding of the lived reality of women in IORA countries by funding research and analysis to develop the evidence base to inform policy decisions and measure progress to achieve gender equality
4. Implement gender responsive policy frameworks and budgets
5. Develop an IORA for responsible tourism to advance women's economic empowerment
6. Take a whole-of-community approach to the women's economic empowerment, acknowledging the complex interaction of gender roles, responsibilities and norms (p. 2)

Following on this, a second event, 'Mobilizing Markets and Commitments to Gender Equality in the Indian Ocean Region' was held in August 2015, in the Republic of Seychelles (IORA, 2015). A report on the Status of Women in the Indian Ocean Rim was launched here, and major themes to emerge from this report were the need for improved education and training for women; rights at work; and the need for access to finance and greater financial independence, or financial inclusion. (UN Women, IORA, DFAT and Government of Seychelles, 2015). The final report, entitled 'Enabling Women's Contributions to the Indian Ocean Rim Economies' (UN Women, 2015), features in the discussion in Priya Chacko's policy paper further in this edition.

We see many of the themes discussed at these IORA events emerge forcefully in this issue of the journal.

We open with Harris-Rimmer, who considers 'womenomics' in the Indian Ocean region, with a focus on trade in textiles and tourism. It is crucial to acknowledge the economic importance of women's participation in informal trade. Harris-Rimmer explores these two sectors and argues that IORA is an important actor in fostering gender equality and in stimulating women's economic empowerment through trade. Whilst recognizing that there are challenges specific to the Indian Ocean region, she finds that IORA can learn from other governance groupings such as APEC and the G20.

The economic significance of women's engagement in informal trade is picked up in an African context by Manjoko and Ranga, who study the informal economy in Zimbabwe, and the effect of structural adjustment programs on Zimbabwean women cross border traders. The study provides a useful picture of these women's circumstances, motivations, and challenges. Despite the contribution of women working in the informal economy to the national economy, the cross border trade is not recognized, and is actively demonised. Important advances can be made to women's empowerment and to the national economy by implementing some policy reforms. These must include ending the 'invisibility' of the cross border trade to policy-makers, the overcoming of a number of minor but influential bureaucratic hurdles, and improving training and education for these women.

Gender bias in policy development is a central theme of Alami and Raharjo's study of fisherwomen in North Sulawesi. The authors map the gender relationship in the fisheries sector, and find that the significant role of women in the primary and secondary sectors of fisheries has been and continues to be undervalued, as a reflection of gender hierarchies. They point to a clear need for the application of a gender lens in policy development, which at the moment is lacking in a gender specific evidence base. This results in a lack of specific policies for women, which could make a significant difference, such as small credit facilities, improved education and training, and an explicit role for women's participation in local communities, such as in local cooperatives.

The education theme is picked up again and explored in the case study of the Solar Mamas, by Giulia Mininni. The Solar Mamas is a training program run by an NGO in rural Rajasthan, which builds and installs solar panels. The program applies a localized, Gandhian approach to knowledge and skills transfer, but which is nevertheless scalable and reproducible. This program has been replicated around the world. Mininni argues that the NGO is playing a key role in transformative agency, whilst acknowledging the difficulty of measuring 'empowerment' of women, the exploring the uneven nature of that empowerment.

Dewi and Yazid also analyze the importance of education, but from another angle: they examine grassroots activism in defence of Indonesian migrant women workers by means of the case studies of three activists. The authors refuse to see these women as passive actors, and they are studied in all their subjectivity. It is a case study of the micro-level, with all its strengths and challenges. This case study speaks to the political decentralization process in Indonesia, which is opening up greater spaces for civil society organizations and social movements. However, Dewi and Yazid argue that 'self and community activities are interrelated.' The authors contend that a central factor in the activists' success, despite the various challenges, is the fact that the women activists are involved from their own experience in migrant work; their personal efforts to educate themselves are also a central theme.

We finish with a general paper, which nevertheless still follows an implicit underlying theme in this edition; of invisibility; otherness; and challenging oppression. In her anthropological piece, Rose Boswell describes the 'voicework' in Sega – a music/dance form with roots in the music of slaves on Indian Ocean islands, and associated with protest against injustice. It is a cultural form inscribed on the UNESCO world heritage list. Examining Sega as practiced in Mauritius and the Seychelles, Boswell finds that Sega gives the islanders voice, and identifies diversity, trangression, and resistance to oppression. Her work encourages scholarship that engages with the senses, and which resists hegemonic othering.

Acknowledgment

This edition of JIOR draws upon the research of a much larger three-year project entitled 'Building an Indian Ocean Region' DP 120101066, which is funded by the Australian Research Council (ARC) Discovery Projects Scheme for funding in 2012–2015. In addition, specific funding for this issue has been generously provided by the Australian Government's Department of Foreign Affairs and Trade.

References

Australian Government. Department of Foreign and Trade. (2014). *Summary report: Path to women's economic empowerment: Tourism and textiles in IORA countries*. Retrieved from http://iora.net/bf/women's-economic-empowerment.aspx

IORA. (2014). *Women's economic empowerment, with a focus on textiles and tourism in the IORA countries*. Park Royal Hotel, Kuala Lumpur, Malaysia. Retrieved December 9, 2016, from http://iora.net/bf/women's-economic-empowerment.aspx

IORA. (2015). *Indian Ocean Rim Association (IORA) Women's economic empowerment event: Mobilizing markets and commitments to gender equality in the Indian ocean rim, Savoy Spa & Resort, Mahé Island, Republic of Seychelles*. Retrieved December 9, 2016, from http://iora.net/bf/women's-economic-empowerment-ii/day-1.aspx

UN Women. (2015). *Enabling women's contributions to the Indian Ocean rim economies*. New York: United Nations. Retrieved December 9, 2016, from http://www.unwomen.org/en/digital-library/publications/2015/9/enabling-womens-contributions-to-the-indian-ocean-rim-economies

UN Women, IORA, DFAT, and Government of Seychelles Conference. (2015). *Enabling women's contributions to Indian Ocean rim economies, Seychelles*. Retrieved December 9, 2016, from http://iora.net/bf/women's-economic-empowerment-ii/day-1.aspx

The future of women's economic empowerment in the Indian Ocean region: governance challenges and opportunities[*]

Susan Harris Rimmer ⓘ

ABSTRACT

This paper seeks to explore the prospects for women's economic empowerment in the Indian Ocean region, bringing a feminist global governance perspective to the priority Trade and Investment Facilitation and Tourism areas of the Indian Ocean Rim Association's (IORA) work. Why would investing in women's economic empowerment bring benefits to 1 billion women living in the IORA region, and how could such investment also benefit 21 IORA economies? Part I outlines the links between women's economic empowerment and overall sustainable macroeconomic growth that reduces inequality. Part II sets out some of the ideas that have been developed in other governance fora, or through international organizations. Part III notes some challenges IORA's leadership may face in pursuing this agenda. I argue that this is an area of great opportunity for IORA, and a test of whether the organization is capable of setting governance and regulatory standards expected of modern regional organizations. Further, this article argues that women are disadvantaged in international trade with a particular focus on Indian Ocean region. Trade governance that gives more precedence to women's rights recognizes women's participation in informal trade and seeks to formalize that participation should be core to the enterprise of IORA.

Introduction

This paper seeks to explore several questions that should be of significance to the leadership of the Indian Ocean Rim Association (IORA). Investing in women's economic empowerment could bring benefits to one billion women living in the IORA region and also benefit 21 IORA economies. IORA can benefit from some of the ideas that have been developed about pathways to women's economic development in other governance settings. IORA can also benefit from the findings of the research of international organizations on the links between women's economic empowerment and overall sustainable macroeconomic growth that reduces inequality. This article argues that women are disadvantaged in

[*]The author was a participant at the IORA Dialogue Event held in Kuala Lumpur from 18 to 20 August 2014. The author is also a member of the MIKTA Academic Network. This paper reflects only the author's views and all errors remain my own. I acknowledge the support of the Australian Research Council through the Future Fellowship. Maps are provided by Cartogis, Australian National University.

international trade with a particular focus on Indian Ocean region. Trade governance that gives more precedence to women's rights, recognizes women's participation in informal trade and seeks to formalize that participation should be core to the enterprise of IORA.

The definition of women's economic empowerment used in this paper has two elements.[1] The first is 'Women's Economic Advancement', meaning economic success and gain for individual women and groups of women based on the skills and resources necessary to compete in markets, plus fair and equal access to economic institutions and second 'Women's Power and Agency', meaning the ability of women to take and act on decisions, and control their own resources and profits. Kabeer (1999) describes empowerment as 'the expansion in people's ability to make strategic life choices in a context where this ability was previously denied to them' (p. 437). I acknowledge economic empowerment is not a proxy for the full range of human rights. Providing women with access to work does not necessarily improve their vulnerability to violence; harmful cultural practices; unfair discrimination or other violations. Many have also argued that women's economic empowerment is also not necessarily feminist in its conceptualization (Cornwall & Rivas, 2015). Nevertheless, this agenda in IORA represents a positive step in using a demographic lens in a progressive way to pursue an economic agenda.

IORA has made several important initial steps to consider women's economic empowerment at the governance level in the last five years. Established in 1997, the IORA Ministers agreed to six priority areas of cooperation in 2011 (see Figure 1: Map of IORA members). These are: maritime safety and security, trade and investment facilitation,

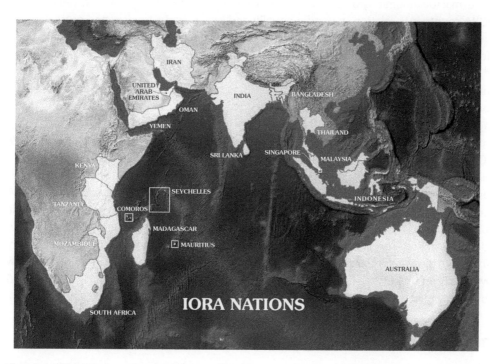

Figure 1. IORA members. Source: Maps produced by CartoGIS (2014). College of Asia and the Pacific, The Australian National University.

fisheries management, disaster risk management, academic and science and technology cooperation, and tourism and cultural exchanges.

The IORA Perth Communiqué 2013 states at paragraph 19:

> The empowerment of women and girls in the region is a high priority for IORA.

This was because the empowerment of women and girls in the region was identified as an important cross-cutting issue for two reasons cited on the IORA website:

> … women have been important contributors to the economic and social development of the countries in the region – a fact that needs to be acknowledged and strengthened within the Association in the future.

> Empowering women and girls is regarded as an essential part of the solution to some of the most serious global challenges of today: food security, poverty reduction and sustainable development. (IORA, 2016)

IORA countries are very diverse, but they have one thing in common. They are seeking sustainable macroeconomic growth and further cooperation. Women's economic participation and agency is one source of macroeconomic growth as per the aims of IORA, and a source of cultural exchange. I consider these issues in relation to the two IORA priorities of trade and investment facilitation; and tourism and cultural exchanges. Notably, IORA also has seven dialogue partners, the most recent being Germany. Some of these partners bring experience in pursuing gender equality in global governance fora and their own foreign policy and can be used as a resource.

Part I outlines the links between women's economic empowerment and overall sustainable macroeconomic growth that reduces inequality. Data snapshots are provided for IORA countries in relation to gender equality indicators, trade, tourism and gross national income (GNI). The IORA region shows great variance in data on gender inequality, GNI, female labor participation and female population.

Part II sets out some of the ideas that have been developed about paths to women's economic development in other governance settings or through the research of international organizations. The benefits of and barriers to women's economic empowerment and agency globally are summarized. Part III notes some of the challenges IORA's leadership may face in pursuing this agenda. As 'womenomics' took the world by storm in 2009, IORA looked decidedly old-fashioned with its lack of female representation and neglect of gender policy. Economic governance should reflect the citizenship of its member states, and it is proven that diverse teams make better decisions.[2] At the same time, IORA Leaders are looking for new pathways to growth, and the headline-stealing economic benefits unlocked by investing in women should make for a persuasive case to IORA decision-makers. The 'size of the prize' for IORA economies for investing in gender equality in growth terms is very large, as is the potential for more sustainable and equal growth. A new McKinsey report puts the figure at US$12 trillion extra gross domestic product (GDP) by 2025 by simply giving more women the same opportunities as men (Woetzel et al., 2015).

Tourism and trade: opportunities for gender initiatives

This growth potential is obvious in case studies chosen for this paper, specifically tourism as a service industry and trade in textiles. Both sectors make significant contributions to economic activity throughout the IORA grouping. Women are active in both sectors, especially as workers, and have the capacity to scale-up their participation. Tourism is a service industry and often a source of foreign currency. It is a focus for IORA due to the common factor of shared access to the Indian Ocean, and the potential for further cooperation and growth. In 2015, tourism contributed 9.8% of world GDP (US$7.2 trillion) and accounted for 284 million jobs (World Travel and Tourism Council [WTTC], 2015). Over the next 10 years this industry is expected to grow by an average of 4% annually, taking it to 10% of global GDP. By 2022, it is anticipated that travel and tourism will account for 328 million jobs; or 1 in every 10 jobs on the planet (WTTC, 2012). Tourism is an industry that has potential to promote the production of local textiles, the protection of heritage sites, and other goods and services that enhance national identity and the broader 'creative economy'. The data presented in Table A1 relates to rates of international arrivals, but there is also considerable economic contribution made by domestic tourism.

Trade is a key area of concern for IORA given its geographic and historic trade routes. All nations, including the IORA Grouping, state that they desire an open, predictable, non-discriminatory and rule-based multilateral trading system centered on the World Trade Organization (WTO). Yet the universal consensus is that the trade system is in deep trouble. The nature of trade itself is changing, the contribution of trade to macroeconomic growth is changing; and the multilateral system is under challenge in terms of trade governance. IORA must work harder to make an impact on the trade agenda, and working harder on 'behind the border' reforms that benefit women could be a way forward. This means we must think about gender issues in relation to a trade agenda which is changing rapidly.

Trade governance

The DNA of trade is changing, with most trade experts urging reforms to the WTO in order to adapt to the new world of global value chains, integrated global standards and transnational investment flows. John Ravenhill has found that international trade increasingly represents trade in components as part of the production of a product. With global manufacturing, goods are now 'made in the world' rather than in a single country. Ravenhill points out that one implication of the rise in global value chains is that traditional trade statistics, which are measured on a gross basis rather than value-added, may be obsolete, and so 'concern over bilateral trade imbalances is clearly misplaced' (Lowy, 2013). Traditional trade policy is no longer an effective tool to assist domestic industries either (Lowy, 2013). Trade in services is a crucial area of liberalization according to almost all economists, but as we enter into a service and knowledge-driven economy this area of negotiations has proven particularly slow and difficult.

The fundamentals of trade are changing. Global trade is growing slower than global production. Trade growth numbers of 3.1% in 2014 and 4% in 2015 may be greater than those of recent years, but they remain significantly lower than long-term average growth rates (Dadush, 2015). Trade deals now often deal with regulatory compatibility between nations (harmonization or mutual recognition) rather than tariff preferences. This includes areas like product standards that more directly affect consumers.

The geo-politics of trade are changing. As the WTO reaches its twentieth anniversary, many member countries are worried about a clash among blocs such as the Brazil, Russia, India, China, South Africa versus the Organization of Economic Cooperation and Development

(OECD) nations. They sometimes face backlash from citizens against some globalization impacts. Important global trade negotiations stall while regional preferential trade agreements proliferate, often likened to noodle bowls or spaghetti. The WTO website lists 282 Regional Trade Agreements in force as of 5 March 2013, and the figure is rising (WTO, 2015).

There are some bright spots on the multilateral trade agenda. A historic WTO agreement on Trade Facilitation reached in December 2013 in Bali aims to make it easier and cheaper for goods to flow through the ports and customs processes of 160 countries. Just before the Group of 20 (G20) Brisbane Summit, the US and India reached a deal that allowed leaders to commit to implement all elements of the Bali package and in June 2015, Australia formally accepted the Agreement on Trade Facilitation. On full implementation, it is estimated it may increase global GDP by US$1 trillion per annum and create 21 million jobs.

WTO Director-General Robert Azevêdo has opened conversations on the future of the 'negotiating pillar' of the WTO: the rules that govern decision-making in the body (Azevedo, 2014). G20 leaders subsequently agreed to discuss ways to make the multilateral trading system work better (G20 Turkey, 2015). Asia Pacific Economic Cooperation (APEC's) decision to liberalize trade in environmental goods and services has been broadly welcomed.

Of course, the WTO has the same great power leadership issues that beset the rest of the multilateral system. The 'emerging economies' are no longer emerging, but have arrived. According to data from the International Monetary Fund (IMF), the combined GDP of the top seven emerging nations is now bigger than those of the conventional Group of Seven industrialized nations when measured in terms of purchasing power parity. The contours of power are almost unrecognizable from 2001 to the present day. In this setting, IORA needs to be creative to make a contribution to trade governance. One opportunity is to focus on improving trade governance and access in certain sectors, and a key area for IORA could be trade in textiles. The total value of textiles exports (fashion, carpets, yarn and wicker-ware) in Indian Ocean Rim economies in 2011–2012 was estimated at $5.5 billion (Department of Foreign Affairs and Trade [DFAT], 2014).

We can think about textiles in a variety of ways in this context: as the expression of cultural and national identity; as part of a production chain that leads to clothing, homewares and other value-added goods; as textiles for export as part of international trade in merchandise or for sale at a local village market stall. Women participate in textiles industries in the IORA grouping in a wide spectrum of roles: as artisans and artists, workers in garment factories, fashion designers, owners of small to medium enterprises, exporters and importers, officials and regulators. In 2011, trade in exports of clothing and textiles contributed over $US706 billion to the global economy. Several IORA countries are major exporters of textiles and clothing.

Finally, IORA is a region that has at least four distinct attributes that make this examination of gender equality significant.

- The region holds over 2 billion people, with over a billion women and girls.
- It is a region that has been woven together by trade routes and sea-lanes for hundreds of years.
- It is still the center of world trade – with the Indian Ocean hosting half the world's container ships at any one time.

- It is a site of immense cultural diversity.

I argue that this region deserves special attention to gender equality issues at a governance level for IORA to become an important regional actor. The IORA grouping could consider advocating for the next round of reforms at the WTO to focus on domestic actions designed to boost women's participation in trade, particularly services such as tourism, trade in particular sectors like textiles.

Key IORA data

Data and rankings are provided for IORA countries about the overall conditions of life for women in Table A1 (Appendix). Notably United Nations Women has created a baseline study to track gender data over time (Marston, 2015). Female populations in IORA are represented visually in Figure 2.

Gender Inequality Indicators are provided by reference to data from the United Nations Development Program Human Development Report. The Gender Inequality Index relies on data from major publicly available databases, including:

- the maternal mortality ratio from the United Nations Maternal Mortality Estimation Group, the WHO, UNICEF, UNFPA and the World Bank;
- adolescent fertility rates from the UN Department of Economic and Social Affair's World Population Prospects;
- educational attainment statistics from the UNESCO Institute for Statistics educational attainment tables and the Barro-Lee data sets;
- parliamentary representation from the International Parliamentary Union and

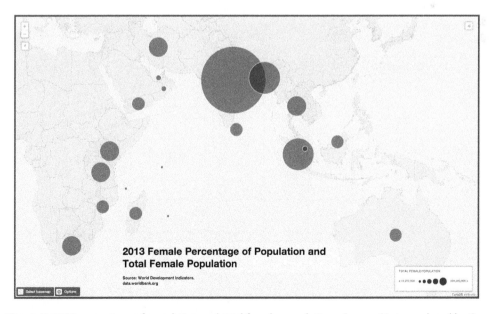

Figure 2. 2013 percentage of population and total female populations. Source: Maps produced by CartoGIS (2014). College of Asia and the Pacific, The Australian National University.

- labor market participation from the International Labor Organization's (ILO) Key Indicators of the Labour Market (KILM) 7th Edition.

The world average score on the GII is 0.463, reflecting a percentage loss in achievement across the three dimensions due to gender inequality of 46.3%.

Trade flows

Table A1 seeks to represent overall trade flows by IORA countries, based on World Bank data. There are some figures for trade in textiles and clothing, but we are looking broadly at merchandise trade as a share of GDP (which is the sum of merchandise exports and imports divided by the value of GDP in 2012 $USD).

We cannot yet present data on trade flows in particular goods or services across the IORA region, but this is a useful ambition for IORA.

Tourism activity

This data in Table A1 is sourced from the World Bank and looks at international arrivals (airports, ports, land borders) in IORA countries in 2010. There is also domestic and regional tourism not captured by this data.

Gross national income

GNI is a measure most are more familiar with, but has a gender impact because it does not generally include unpaid care work, which is undertaken mainly by women all around the globe. The variation between IORA members is stark (Figure 3).

Figure 3. IORA GDP 2012. Source: Maps produced by CartoGIS (2014). College of Asia and the Pacific, The Australian National University.

Female labor force participation rates

This is an important area to be concerned with data and evidence, as it is key to arguments about economic growth for the nation as a whole, so we have pulled it out of the general focus on gender inequality. Our map is based on data collected by the World Bank (UNDP, 2013), and the KILM 7th Edition.

Part II: women's economic empowerment: benefits and barriers

The World Bank has identified that the common constraints facing many women in participating in the formal economy include lack of mobility, time due to unpaid care work, skills, exposure to violence and the absence of basic legal rights (2012). All economic data tells us that tourism is a source of growth, trade, especially in clothing is a source of growth, and that investing in women is a source of growth, as well as a fulfilment of human rights and social potential.

Benefits

Women make up a little over half the world's population, but their contribution to measured economic activity, growth and well-being is considered by mainstream economic institutions to be below its potential. This has led to the inclusion of gender-specific targets and indicators in the newly agreed 17 Sustainable Development Goals as part of the 2030 Development Agenda (Goals 5, 8 and 10 in particular). There is settled research that focusing on women in development and poverty-reduction programs had overall benefits for the target community.

There is also international legal commitment through treaty law to the rights and status of women. The Convention for the Elimination of All Forms of Discrimination Against Women was adopted by the UN General Assembly in 1979 and now has 187 state parties. All IORA states have signed except Iran. The Convention contains a broad definition of discrimination in Article 1, covering both equality of opportunity (formal equality) and equality of outcome (de facto or substantive equality):

> [D]iscrimination against women violates the principles of equality of rights and respect for human dignity, is an obstacle to the participation of women, on equal terms with men, in the political, social, economic and cultural life of their countries, hampers the growth of the prosperity of society and the family and makes more difficult the full development of the potentialities of women in the service of their countries and of humanity.

The Convention requires states to take legal and other measures to ensure the practical realization of the principle of sex equality (Article 2). The Convention covers a broad range of areas where state parties must work to eliminate discrimination.[3] Article 4 allows for affirmative action, in the form of temporary special measures designed to accelerate de facto equality such as quotas in employment, education, financial services and politics to overcome historical barriers. Despite this, the World Bank found recently that in 100 economies, women face gender-based job restrictions under the law. Most IORA members have significant legal barriers to women's participation in work and public life (World Bank, 2016).

The major global economic institutions have been providing evidence since 2006 that when women are able to develop their full labor market potential, there can be significant macroeconomic gains for the nation (Elborgh-Woytek et al., 2013). Some studies have put the figure as high as a 27% increase for some regions (Aguirre, Hoteit, Rupp, & Sabbagh, 2012). It is not just the quantum of growth that interests economists but the quality of the growth.

The *World development report 2012: Gender equality and development* released by the World Bank urged states to close differences in access to economic opportunities and the ensuing earnings and productivity gaps between women and men. The Bank advocates increasing access to child care and early childhood development, and investing in rural women (World Bank, 2012). These are social policy recommendations, but driven by an economic growth goal.

These World Bank studies usually focus on the potential of female labor force participation. Between 1980 and 2008, 52 million women joined the labor force, which equates to 52% of all workers globally. Men's participation rates declined from 82% in 1980 to 78% in 2008.[4] The rise in female labor force participation can be attributed to rising education levels, economic development, anti-discrimination measures and declining fertility rates.

'Womenomics' is posited to have several overall macro benefits:

- Some argue that higher female work force participation would also result in a more skilled labor force, in view of women's higher education levels (Steinberg & Nakane, 2012).
- Studies have shown that women in developing countries are more likely than men to invest a large proportion of their household income in the education of their children. According to the ILO, women's work, both paid and unpaid, may be the single most important poverty-reducing factor in developing economies (Heintz, 2013).
- The benefits can be very large in scale. Detailed studies have modelled that increasing the female workforce participation in developed economies such as Australia, using the same policy measures that our comparator Canada has successfully implemented (tax, welfare reform and affordable childcare), would add $AUD25 billion to Australia's GDP (Daley, McGannon, & Ginnivan, 2012, p. 39).

There is significant evidence that supports the formal and informal education of women and girls as the foundation for women's participation in the formal economy in the longer term. As the Australian Minister for Women Michaelia Cash stated at the UN in 2014: 'Education is the anti-poverty vaccine for women'.[5]

Other benefits of women's economic empowerment for economic governance need more research. The employment of women on an equal basis should allow companies to make better use of the available talent pool, with potential growth implications (Barsh & Yee, 2012). There is evidence (contested) of a positive impact of women's presence on boards and in senior management on companies' performance. Companies employing female managers are likely to be better positioned to serve consumer markets dominated by women (OECD, 2012).

There might also be better corporate governance (OECD, 2012) and risk management (Coates & Herbert, 2008) from more diversity on boards. As IMF head Lagarde (2011) famously said:

> Gender-dominated environments are not good … particularly in the financial sector where there are too few women. In gender-dominated environments, men have a tendency to … show how hairy chested they are, compared with the man who's sitting next to them. I honestly think that there should never be too much testosterone in one room.

Barriers

Despite these benefits, female labor force participation has remained lower than male participation, and in several nations, the rates are in decline. Where women are represented, it is not at leadership levels. UN Women found that in 'most Indian Ocean Rim Member States, women are significantly underrepresented in management, senior management and leadership positions in the private sector, cooperatives and trade unions' (Marston, 2015, p. 20).

Barriers to women's economic empowerment include the following:

- Women do the majority of unpaid work especially in areas of care and domestic labor.
- When women are employed in paid work, they are overrepresented in the informal sector with temporary or precarious working arrangements.
- Women also face significant wage differentials vis-à-vis their male colleagues.
- In many countries, legal, social and cultural barriers to joining the labor market restrict women's options for paid work.
- Female representation in public and private sector leadership positions and on boards, as well as rates of female entrepreneurship remains low.
- Women are in occupational segregation with high risk during transition to international markets – women are concentrated in sectors, industries, occupations and jobs with lower average productivity.
- Women often have lower level education and literacy rates.
- Women often do unpaid work rarely gets recognition at a societal level.
- Women experience more obstacles in accessing land, financial services, technology, information, other productive resources and markets.
- Approximately one in three women experience violence in their private and public lives.[6]

The UN Women report found significant evidence of these barriers in IORA member countries in its recent academic study (Marston, 2015).

Trade barriers

Evidence shows that international trade tends to increase the availability of formal but mostly low-skilled, labor-intensive and low value-added jobs in developing countries, with most of these jobs in export-oriented having been filled by women in recent decades. Many women are also involved in informal trade.

The UN states:

> Measures such as access to credit, social safety nets – such as health insurance – transport, foreign currency exchange, infrastructure for storage of goods, refrigeration of agricultural commodities and transport facilities, as well as access to health care, water and sanitation facilities and security services, and training of customs and police officers about women's rights, would greatly improve informal traders' activity and enhance their contribution to wealth creation and poverty reduction. (UN Womenwatch, 2011)

The UN has found that important structural barriers are preventing women to benefit from trade-orientation; these include: women and girls' limited access to education and skills, including in cutting-edge educational fields; de jure and de facto discrimination against women in the control over economic and financial resources, productive assets and access to financial services; and women's limited access to new technologies for production, training, information and marketing.

Trade policy should thus consider how it can enable women to become key actors in those sectors of the economy that benefit most from trade; it should provide development pathways for women into more technologically advanced and dynamic sectors of the economy; and account for the likely effects of widening or closing the gender wage gap and reducing women's time poverty.

The UN women report on IORA found that:

> Women entrepreneurs are on the rise in many Indian Ocean Rim countries and could make an important contribution to national economies. Countries that have not yet created enabling environments to support women entrepreneurs would greatly benefit from doing so. While women make important contributions to a range of supply chains across Indian Ocean Rim economies, significant efforts are still needed to better integrate them into these chains and move them into higher value-added production and decision-making positions. (Marston, 2015, p. 20)

Tourism barriers

According to the *Global report on women in tourism*, tourism is one of the world's largest generators of wealth and employment, and provides a wide range of income-generation opportunities for women, particularly in developing regions. Women are almost twice as likely to be employers in tourism as compared to others sectors. Tourism also offers leadership possibilities, with women accounting for one in five tourism ministers worldwide; more than in any other branch of government.

Nevertheless, women are often concentrated in low-skill, low-paid and precarious jobs, typically earn 10–15% less than their male counterparts, and tend to perform jobs such as cooking, cleaning and hospitality (UN Women, 2010) which conform to societal roles for many cultures.

The next section examines what other comparator governance forums are doing to deal with similar challenges in their membership.

Part III: building equity into trade governance

This Part outlines the current measures being undertaken by comparator governance groupings that have a similar focus on economic growth. Groupings that have some overlap with IORA in terms of diverse groupings include APEC, the G20 and Mexico,

Indonesia, Korea, Turkey, Australia (MIKTA). Notably, the International Trade Center in Geneva as part of the WTO has launched a 'She Trades' initiative with a comprehensive policy program attached (https://www.shetrades.com/), in order to assist international organizations with this agenda (2015).

Asia-Pacific economic cooperation

The first APEC Ministerial Meeting on Women was held in Manila in 1998, which paved the way for the drafting of the Framework for the Integration of Women in the APEC agenda, followed by Guidelines.[7] APEC Women and the Economy Forums have been held as High Level meetings since 1998. The Policy Partnership on Women and the Economy (PPWE) was established at the second Senior Officials' Meeting in May 2011 held at Big Sky, Montana, the United States in the lead up to the 2011 San Francisco Declaration at the High Level Policy Dialogue on Women and the Economy. The PPWE is a single public-private entity to streamline and elevate the influence of women's issues within APEC, supported by the Secretariat.

APEC has also created platforms to gather good quality diagnostic data for policy influence, such as the APEC women and the economy dashboard.[8] APEC also showcases good gender practice and the good practices of women and men, companies and government programs committed to gender inclusive growth. One APEC example is the site www.we-apec.com focused on increasing the numbers and success of female entrepreneurs. Generally APEC is cited as a relatively successful organization in terms of gender mainstreaming (True, 2008). The APEC Private–Public Dialogue on Women and the Economy is innovative, strategic and seems capable of having policy influence on leaders.

MIKTA

MIKTA is a relatively new grouping of foreign ministers from five systematically important economies, which began in September 2013.[9] MIKTA sees itself as a 'cross-regional consultative platform' that aims to be a 'bona fide enabler in terms of providing global public goods' through global governance reform (MIKTA Ministers, 2015; MIKTA Vision Statement).

The MIKTA group releases joint statements such as celebrating International Women's Day at the UN in Geneva (MIKTA, 2015a). They have also agreed to use their combined clout in other economic fora such as the G20 to achieve gender equality outcomes at a strategic level:

> 9. We agreed to work together to promote gender equality by advocating in our respective regions broader acceptance of the commitment to reduce the gender gap in employment by 25 per cent by 2025, taking into account national circumstances. We will also encourage gender equality across the spectrum of MIKTA activities. (MIKTA, 2015b)

MIKTA is still a new entity, but it clear that IORA or parts of IORA could create a similar nimble grouping that seeks to improve governance outcomes by coordinated, timely action in particular areas of interest.

The G20

The G20 has made incremental progress on gender equality issues as the 'premier forum for macroeconomic cooperation'. The G20 leaders have committed to:

- helping achieve progress on the G20's commitments to 'women's full economic and social participation', which was made in the Los Cabos Leaders' Declaration in 2012 (G20 Mexico);
- 'women's financial inclusion and education', which was made in the St Petersburg Leaders' Declaration in 2013 (G20 Russia), and the Women's Finance Hub. The Global Partnership for Financial Inclusion and the G20 Financial Inclusion Indicators initiated in Seoul were launched in 2012 and [10]
- 'reducing the gap in participation rates between men and women by 25 per cent by 2025', which was agreed on in the Brisbane Leaders' Declaration in 2014, and which would, if implemented, create 100 million new jobs for women (G20 Australia, 2014).

The female labor participation target represents a step forward for the G20, which has no secretariat and operates by domestic action coordinated with other members, supported by the international financial institutions.

Like APEC, G20 Leaders have established official second track processes to aid their deliberations. Under the 2015 Turkish G20 Presidency, the W20 engagement group was officially established to provide policy advice to G20 Leaders (Harris Rimmer, 2015). It was launched in Ankara on 6 September 2015 and the first summit took place on 15–16 October 2015. The Istanbul W20 communiqué made recommendations in areas of empowering women through strengthening linkages between education, employment and entrepreneurship; increasing the number of women in leadership positions; ensuring women's access to finance and supporting women's networks and women owned enterprises (W20, 2015). The 2015 process was influenced by an open poll and delegate submissions, and proposed a monitoring system for future W20 Summits.

China continued Turkey's investment in the W20 in 2016, chiefly through the W20 Summit in Xi'an where the representatives of G20 countries and invited guests agreed a communiqué to be presented to the G20 Leaders in the lead up to the September 2016 Hangzhou Summit (W20 China, 2016). China had some experience in this area having held a successful APEC Women in the Economy Forum in 2015 with discussions on women and green development, as well as women and regional trade. The All-China Women's Federation hosted the 2016 W20 Summit with a keynote speech by China's Vice President, Li Yuanchao. Li opened the summit in Xi'an on 26 May 2016 and his speech demonstrated the increasing legitimacy of the gender and growth agenda, which the Chinese term 'She-Power':

> It is all the more important to pool women's wisdom and strength at a time when the global economic recovery remains fragile. As the Chinese economy moves into a New Normal, efforts are made to encourage mass innovation and entrepreneurship, and women are essential in this endeavour. (China Daily, 2016)

The G20 itself and the engagement groups are supported by the international financial institutions, as noted. The IMF and OECD have been exceptionally supportive of the W20, as has UN Women (an entity responsible for promoting women's empowerment and gender equality) and the ILO. For example, the OECD held a panel in June 2016 on the G20 labor gap target (OECD, 2016). These organizations are also involved with a new initiative called the High Level Panel on Women's Economic Empowerment, led by UN Women, funded by Canada and the UK. The inaugural meeting of the Panel was held on 15 March 2016 in the UN headquarters in New York. The Panel is expert and not country based. This high level attention by the leading economies and corresponding UN action is a welcome development, but is still to be tested in improved results within G20/ UN members.

Part IV: challenges to IORA's leadership

The IORA Grouping has a great opportunity to draw on the lessons learned in this area by other governance groupings. IORA leaders could send a clear signal in their political declarations that investing in over a billion women in the IORA region could lead to sustainable growth. The IORA website sets the policy parameters leaders can consider, and they reflect the various modalities adopted by the groupings above:

- a clear policy framework;
- more rigorous gender analysis of policy initiatives across the IORA agenda;
- particular policy reforms directed at particular barriers, such as education;
- the collection of better quality comparable data and data analysis;
- collaboration with other organizations and groupings and
- stakeholder engagement.[11]

One initial stakeholder event was held in 2014 in Kuala Lumpur, under the auspices of Australia. Representatives from all 21 IORA economies were asked for six key messages for the leaders meeting in Perth on how best to support women's economic empowerment in Indian Ocean rim economies. An interesting outcome was how clearly participants wanted acknowledgement of their economic contribution by the regional leaders and gender mainstreaming of current initiatives.

(1) Invest in women's education, professional development and training.
(2) Promote national cultural identity – self, product and place – in a way that encompasses the strengths and contribution of women.
(3) Contribute to broader understanding of the lived reality of women in IORA countries by funding research and analysis to develop the evidence-base to inform policy decisions and measure progress to achieve gender equality.
(4) Implement gender responsive policy frameworks and budgets.
(5) Develop an IORA framework for responsible tourism to advance women's economic empowerment.
(6) Take a whole-of-community approach to the women's economic empowerment, acknowledging the complex interaction of gender roles, responsibilities and norms (DFAT, 2014).

There are also reforms IORA could make in this area to provide the basis for incremental reforms over time that are not onerous or expensive. IORA could create a more specific version of APEC Public Private Dialogue or the W20, such as an 'Expert group on IORA Women in Trade', or an 'Expert group on Women in Tourism'. Alternatively, each existing national trade advisory group or tourism council could nominate a female member to liaise with a new IORA network. IORA countries could consider appointing national champions and special IORA envoys for women's entrepreneurship (based on Sweden) that meet and share best practice. Or, like APEC, the IORA Grouping could create new awards for women.

This focus on including the business community has strong antecedents. The Perth IORA meeting was preceded by 'IORA Business Week' focused on regional trade that was well received (Bergin, 2014). The Perth meeting also saw the launch of an IORA Economic Declaration focused on 'blue economy'. It does contain the encouraging phrase: '[t]he prosperity of the region will only be realised fully by investing in the empowerment of women'.[12] A fund of one million dollars to support economic diplomacy initiatives and activities in the Indian Ocean region was established last year, any modest investment in women's economic empowerment is likely to reap dividends for the IORA Grouping.

It is clear there is no restriction on the modalities or issues IORA could focus on to increase economic growth through women's economic empowerment. In the next section I consider challenges for the IORA grouping in this area.

Part V: implications for the region and for IORA

The IORA Council of Ministers' meeting in Perth, Australia in October 2014 struggled to follow up its commitment to gender issues from the 2013 Communiqué, expressing only their pleasure in successful stakeholder events without any new commitments. The diversity of the membership is an obvious challenge, but other groupings like MIKTA, APEC and the G20 have the same issues with diversity. The variation between average income between countries and disparity in stages of economic development is also seen in the G20 but G20 members tend to have more geo-political weight as well as economic clout. It is a regional grouping, but spread across a vast geographic area, similar to APEC. There has long been a sense that the increasing strategic importance of the Indian Ocean needs to be matched by the strength of its regional governance grouping (Rudd, 2011). But there is a history and distinct outlook for those nations bounded by the Indian Ocean – Bose (2006) reminds us how a region's culture, economy, politics and imagination are woven together in time and place.

One obvious challenge to pursuing a women's economic empowerment agenda in the IORA grouping is the low leaders of female representation at leader level. Official IORA 'family photos' reveal only 20% women (5 out of 25 delegates) at best; at worst, no women can be seen at some of the meetings over the last decade. There are less obvious, but similar issues at the officials level. Women's voices generally are not heard in senior officials and ministerial meetings, leading to failure to reach consensus on adopting an IORA policy on gender equality in 2015. This is not unique to IORA, nor does it prevent leaders taking on this agenda successfully but is notable.

Another issue specific to this agenda is the extreme variation on the Gender Equality Index between members of the IORA Grouping. Usually a foundational step for regional groupings is to establish comparable data. In this case, viewing gender-disaggregated data in a comparable setting can be a sensitive issue for states. Another layer to the data issue is that analysis of the barriers to women's economic empowerment for the purposes of macroeconomic growth inevitably draws the eye to structural exclusions and human rights issues.

One answer might be to choose the data gap carefully with this sensitivity in mind. The IORA Grouping could support countries in collecting and analyzing sex-disaggregated data related to informal traders for example, using a participatory methodology to explore what women themselves identify as hurdles to their participation in the formal economy. Alternatively, the IORA Grouping could establish a baseline for comparable quality data on women engaged in the tourism sector in IORA countries.

At the UN, the ILO is a key actor in trade issues. Even the G20 as an informal summit has the L20 engagement group with a very influential role. The potential role of labor and their collective voice has not been a feature of IORA deliberations. Ruwanpura (2016) argues that governance regimes show partiality towards firm-oriented (i.e. capital) solutions:

> Global governance regimes then requires acknowledging how the state explicitly or implicitly sides with capital over labour or vice versa at different historical junctures—and how this evolving landscape shapes has important consequences for labour gains or losses and the partiality of this capitalist development process. In the absence of such recognition, the silent role of the state in global initiatives is deafening .... (p. 441)

This means that IORA should take a triumvirate approach, where active efforts should be made to include the voices of female workers and labor organizations, as well as attempts to increase women's representation as trade officials, and in chambers of commerce.

In terms of the structural issues, the IORA Grouping could acknowledge in future official documents that there is broader foundation for women's economic empowerment, and that overall IORA countries could strive to improve the employment conditions, access and quality of jobs including in the informal economy and promote family-friendly policies and workplace practices to ensure that both women and men are able to maximize their productivity, and have access to social protection benefits.

A final challenge is that economic issues are often eclipsed in the world of high politics by security issues, and maritime security will no doubt remain the top of IORA's priorities for the immediate future.

Conclusion

This paper sought to explore several questions that should be of significance to the leadership of the IORA and the future direction of the Grouping. This study has shown that empowerment of women and girls in the region was correctly identified as an important cross-cutting issue for the IORA Grouping, as equal contributors to the prosperity of the region thus far, and a key part of further progress. The two IORA priorities of trade and investment facilitation; and tourism were considered in terms of productive investments in gender equality.

Part I outlined uncontested evidence from international financial institutions that investing in women's economic empowerment will bring benefits to one billion women living in the IORA region and also benefit 21 IORA economies, while reducing general inequality. Part II examined how other governance groupings such as MIKTA, G20 and especially APEC have provided lessons on developing paths to women's economic development through successful initiatives and policy attention.

Part III noted some of the challenges IORA's leadership may face in pursuing this agenda; including data sensitivity, leadership and the dominance of a security lens. These challenges are real, but can be overcome. As 'womenomics' took the world by storm in 2009, IORA has started to look decidedly old-fashioned with its lack of female representation and neglect of gender policy, and thereby out of touch with current economic thinking. The 'blue ocean economy' of the Indian Ocean Rim could and should have stewards of both sexes. This is an area of great opportunity for IORA, and a test of whether the organization is capable of setting the governance and regulatory standards expected of modern regional organizations that are proven pathways to reach its stated goals.

Notes

1. There is no accepted definition of women's economic empowerment in international law as yet, and there are a variety of ways the phrase is used by the UN, the OECD, the World Bank and states. The definition used in this paper using the two elements of success and power is based on the report by the International Center for Research on Women by Gollo, Malhotra, Nanda, and Mehra (2011). They state at p. 4: 'A woman is economically empowered when she has both the ability to succeed and advance economically and the power to make and act on economic decisions.'
2. See further Galinsky et al. (2015) and Lückerath-Rovers (2013).
3. These provisions include political and public life (Article 7), international organizations (Article 8), education (Article 10), employment (Article 11), health care (Article 12), financial credit (Article 13b), cultural life (Article 13c), the rural sector (Article 14), the law (Article 15) and marriage (Article 16).
4. A visual representation can be seen here: http://go.worldbank.org/9V87N19PJ0.
5. Response to question at the UN Commission for the Status of Women 58 side event on Gender Equality in Education, March 2014.
6. See generally 'Women in the Economy', Platform For Action, The United Nations Fourth World Conference on Women, Beijing, China – September 1995, available at http://www.un.org/womenwatch/daw/beijing/platform/economy.htm.
7. See further the APEC 'Gender Issues' site: http://www.apec.org/Home/Groups/SOM-Steering-Committee-on-Economic-and-Technical-Cooperation/Working-Groups/Policy-Partnership-on-Women-and-the-Economy.
8. Available at https://www.microlinks.org/sites/default/files/resource/files/apec-women-and-the-economy-dashboard-framework.pdf.
9. See further the official MIKTA website: http://www.mikta.org.
10. See further the official GPFI website at http://www.gpfi.org/about-gpfi.
11. See further IORA/Gender at http://www.iora.net/about-us/priority-areas/gender-empowerment.aspx.
12. See further http://www.iora.net/media/151280/iora_economic_declaration.pdf.

Disclosure statement

No potential conflict of interest was reported by the author.

Funding

This work was supported by the Australian Research Council FT140100084.

ORCID

Susan Harris Rimmer http://orcid.org/0000-0002-6455-9546

References

Aguirre, D., Hoteit, L., Rupp, C., & Sabbagh, K. (2012). *Empowering the third billion. Women and the world of work in 2012*. San Francisco: Booz and Company.

Azevedo, R. (2014, December 10). *Let's make sure 2015 will be a year to remember for the WTO*. Speech to WTO General Council. Retrieved from http://www.wto.org/english/news_e/news14_e/gc_rpt_10dec14_e.htm

Barsh, J., & Yee, L. (2012). Unlocking the full potential of women at work. *McKinsey & Company/Wall Street Journal* Retrieved from http://www.mckinsey.com/business-functions/organization/our-insights/unlocking-the-full-potential-of-women-at-work.

Bergin, A. (2014, October 16). The Indian Ocean Rim Association: A progress report. ASPI Strategist. Retrieved from https://www.aspistrategist.org.au/the-indian-ocean-rim-association-a-progress-report/.

Bose, S. (2006). *A hundred horizons: The Indian Ocean in the age of global empire*. Cambridge: Harvard University Press.

China Daily. (2016, May 25). *Remarks by Vice-President Li Yuanchao promote women's equal participation and foster innovative development of the world economy*. Opening Ceremony of the W20 Meeting, Xi'an. Retrieved from http://www.chinadaily.com.cn/china/2016-05/26/content_25474918.htm

Coates, J. M., & Herbert, J. (2008). Endogenous steroids and financial risk taking on a London trading floor. *Proceedings of the National Academy of Sciences, 105*(15), 6167–6172.

Cornwall, A., & Rivas, A.-M. (2015). From 'gender equality and 'women's empowerment' to global justice: Reclaiming a transformative agenda for gender and development. *Third World Quarterly*, *36*(2), 369–415.

Dadush, U. (2015). What should be done about the great trade slowdown? *CEIP op ed*. Retrieved August 19, from http://carnegieendowment.org/2015/08/19/what-should-be-done-about-great-trade-slowdown/iew5

Daley, J., McGannon, C., & Ginnivan, L. (2012). *Game-changers: Economic reform priorities for Australia*. Melbourne: Grattan Institute.

Department of Foreign Affairs and Trade. (2014). *Paths to women's economic empowerment: Tourism and textiles in IORA countries*. Canberra: Government of Australia. Retrieved from http:// www.iora. net/media/149928/australian_hosted_iora_event_on_women_s_economic_empowerment_17-19_august_2014.pdf

Elborgh-Woytek, K., Newiak, M., Kochhar, K., Fabrizio, S., Kpodar, K., Wingender, P., … Schwartz, G. (2013, September). *Women, work, and the economy: Macroeconomic gains from gender equity*. IMF staff discussion note. Retrieved June 2, 2014, from https://www.imf.org/external/pubs/ft/ sdn/2013/sdn1310.pdf

G20 Australia. (2014, November 15–16). *G20 Australia leaders' communiqué*. Brisbane. Retrieved from http://www.g20australia.org/sites/default/files/g20_resources/library/brisbane_g20_leaders_ summit_communique.pdf

G20 Mexico. (2012, June 18–19). *G20 Mexico leaders' declaration*. Los Cabos. Retrieved from http:// g20watch.edu.au/g20-leaders-declaration-los-cabos-2012

G20 Russia. (2013, September 5). *G20 Russia leaders' declaration*. St Petersburg. Retrieved from http:// www.mofa.go.jp/files/000013493.pdf

G20 Turkey. (2015, May). *Prospects for global trade*. IMF and World Bank. Retrieved from http://g20. org/English/Documents/PastPresidency/201512/t20151228_2060.html

Galinsky, A., Todd, A. R., Homan, A. C., Phillips, K. W., Apfelbaum, E. P., Sasaki, S. J., … Maddux, W. W. (2015, November). Maximizing the gains and minimizing the pains of diversity: A policy perspective. *Perspectives on Psychological Science, 10*, 742–748.

Global partnership for financial inclusion. Retrieved March 1, 2016, from http://www.gpfi.org/about-gpfi

Gollo, A. M., Malhotra, A., Nanda, P., & Mehra, R. (2011). *Understanding and measuring women's economic empowerment: Definition, framework and indices*. Washington, DC: The International Center for Research on Women.

Heintz, J. (2013, March). *Missing women: The G20, gender equality and global economic governance*. Report for the Heinrich Böll Stiftung Foundation. Washington, DC: Heinrich Böll Stiftung.

International Trade Center. (2015). *Call to action – she trades*. Retrieved from http://www.intracen. org/uploadedFiles/intracenorg/Content/Redesign/Contact_Us/Call%20to%20Action%20-%20One %20million%20women-owned%20businesses%20in%20the%20market%20by%20202 … .pdf

IORA website. *Gender empowerment*. Retrieved from http://www.iora.net/about-us/priority-areas/ gender-empowerment.aspx

Kabeer, N. (1999). Resources, agency, achievements: Reflections on the measurement of women's empowerment. *Development and Change, 30*, 435–464. doi:10.1111/1467-7660.00125

Lagarde, C. (2011, February 7). There should never be too much testosterone in one room. *The Independent*.

Lowy Institute. (2013, June 2). *G20 monitor: Trade and the G20*. Retrieved from http://www. lowyinstitute.org/publications/trade-and-g20

Lückerath-Rovers, M. (2013, May). Women on boards and firm performance. *Journal of Management & Governance, 17*(2), 491–509.

Marston, A. (2015). *'Enabling women's contributions to the Indian Ocean rim economies' UN Women*. Retrieved from http://www.unwomen.org/en/digital-library/publications/2015/9/enabling-wome ns-contributions-to-the-indian-ocean-rim-economies#sthash.4Vt8D0FV.dpuf

MIKTA. (2015a, March 9). *Joint statement on the occasion of commemorating international women's day at the 28th session of the Human Rights Council, Geneva*. Retrieved form http://www.mikta. org/document/others.php?pn=1&sn=&st=&sc=&sd=&sdate=&edate=&sfld=&sort=&at=view&idx =109

MIKTA. (2015b, September 26). *Joint communiqué: 6th MIKTA foreign ministers' meeting*. New York. Retrieved from http://www.mikta.org/document/joint.php?pn=1&sn=&st=&sc=&sd=&sdate=&edate=&sfld=&sort=&at=view&idx=160

MIKTA Ministers. (2015, January 7). Mr. Yun Byung-se, Minister of Foreign Affairs, the Republic of Korea; Mr. José Antonio Meade Kuribreña, Secretary of Foreign Affairs of Mexico; Ms. Retno L. P. Marsudi, Foreign Minister of Indonesia; Mr. Mevlüt Çavuşoğlu, Minister of Foreign Affairs of Turkey; and Ms. Julie Bishop, Minister of Foreign Affairs and Trade of Australia. (2015). *Opinion editorial: '21st century global governance: Rise of the rest – cross-regional networks'*. Retrieved from http://foreignminister.gov.au/articles/Pages/2015/jb_ar_150107.aspx?ministerid=4

OECD. (2012). *Women's economic empowerment*. The OECD DAC Network on Gender Equality (Gendernet). Retrieved June 1, 2014, from www.oecd.org/dac/povertyreduction/50157530.pdf

OECD Forum. (2016). *Closing the gender gap: 25 by 2025*. Retrieved from http://webcastcdn.viewontv.com/client/oecd/forum2016/video_33304388ad3a42c49a38e79179ffe46e.html

Rimmer, S. H. (2015, November 10). *Why the W20? Reasons to take the newest g20 social partner seriously*. Retrieved from http://www.usak.org.tr/en/usak-analysis/comments/why-the-w20-reasons-to-take-the-newest-g20-social-partner-seriously

Rudd, K. (2011, November 14). The Indian Ocean: In need of a regional organisation to match its growing influence. *The Hindu*.

Ruwanpura, K. N. (2016). Garments without guilt? Uneven labour geographies and ethical trading – Sri Lankan labour perspectives. *Journal of Economic Geography, 16*(2), 423–446.

Steinberg, C., & Nakane, M. (2012). *Can women save Japan? IMF Working Paper 2012*. Retrieved from https://www.imf.org/external/pubs/ft/wp/2012/wp12248.pdf

True, J. (2008). Gender mainstreaming and trade governance in the Asia-Pacific Economic Cooperation forum (APEC). In G. Waylen & S. Rai (Eds.), *Global governance: Feminist perspectives* (pp. 129–159). New York: Palgrave.

UNDP. (2013). *Human development indicators report 2013*. Retrieved from http://hdr.undp.org/en/2013-report

UN Women. (2010). *Global report on women in tourism 2010*. Retrieved from http://www.unwomen.org/~/media/Headquarters/Media/Stories/en/folletoglobarlreportpdf.pdf

UN Womenwatch. (2011). *Gender equality & trade policy*. Retrieved from http://www.un.org/womenwatch/feature/trade/gender_equality_and_trade_policy.pdf

W20. (2015). *Women's summit communiqué, G20 Turkey*. Retrieved October 17, 2015, from http://www.g20.utoronto.ca/2015/151017-w20.html.

W20 China. (2016). Retrieved from http://www.womenofchina.com.cn/html/report/9639-1.htm

Woetzel, J., Madgavkar, A., Ellingrud, K., Labaye, E., Devillard, S., Kutcher, E., … Krishnan, M. (2015, September). *How advancing women's equality can add $12 trillion to global growth*. Mckinsey Global Institute. Retrieved from http://www.mckinsey.com/global-themes/employment-and-growth/how-advancingwomens-equality-can-add-12-trillion-to-global-growth

World Bank. (2012). *World development report 2012: Gender equality and development*. Retrieved from http://econ.worldbank.org/WBSITE/EXTERNAL/EXTDEC/EXTRESEARCH/EXTWDRS/EXTWDR2

World Bank. (2016). *Women, business and the law 2016*. Retrieved from http://wbl.worldbank.org/~/media/WBG/WBL/Documents/Reports/2016/Women-Business-and-the-Law-2016.pdf

World Trade Organization. (2012). *International trade statistics 2012*. Retrieved June 1, 2014, from www.wto.org/english/res_e/statis_e/its2012_e/its2012_e.pdf

World Trade Organization. (2015). *Regional trade agreements information system*. Retrieved March 5, 2016, from http://rtais.wto.org/ui/PublicAllRTAList.aspx

World Travel and Tourism Council, Travel & Tourism Economic Impact. (2012). Retrieved from http://www.wttc.org/site_media/uploads/downloads/world2012.pdf

World Travel and Tourism Council, Travel & Tourism Economic Impact. (2015). Retrieved from http://www.wttc.org/research/economic-research/economic-impact-analysis/

Appendix

Table A1. IORA by the numbers.

	GDP per capita 2012	Tourism – International arrivals 2010	Trade in Merchandise (WTO, 2012)	Gender inequality index 2012
Australia	34,548	5,885,000	33.8	0.115/rank 2
Bangladesh	1568	303,000	51.1	0.518/rank 146
Comoros	980	15,000	54.5	Rank 169
India	3203	5,776,000	42.1	0.61/rank 136
Indonesia	4094	7,003,000	43.2	0.494/rank 121
Iran	10.462	2,938,000	30.2	0.496/rank 76
Kenya	1507	1,470,000	55.7	0.608/rank 145
Madagascar	853	196,000	46	Rank 151
Malaysia	13,672	24,577,000	139	0.256/rank 64
Mauritius	12,737	935,000	68.6	0.377/rank 80
Mozambique	861	1,718,000	75.8	0.582/rank 185
Oman	25,330	1,048,000	103.5	0.34/rank 84
Seychelles	23,172	175,000	125.6	Rank 46
Singapore	53,591	9,161,000	274.7	0.101/rank 18
South Africa	9678	8,074,000	54.9	0.462/rank 121
Sri Lanka	4929	654,000	48.1	0.402/rank 92
Tanzania	1334	754,000	58.8	0.566/rank 152
Thailand	7633	15,936,000	130.4	0.36/rank 103
United Arab Emirates	42,293	–	135.5	0.241/rank 41
Yemen	2060	1,025,000	64.1	0.747/ rank 160

Note: Data snapshot taken at the year with the most comparable data.

Opportunities and challenges faced by women involved in informal cross-border trade in the city of Mutare during a prolonged economic crisis in Zimbabwe

Caroline Manjokoto and Dick Ranga

ABSTRACT

This paper assessed the opportunities and challenges faced by women involved in informal cross-border trade (ICBT) in Mutare during a prolonged economic crisis in Zimbabwe. Sixteen women informal cross-border traders were interviewed in depth while two cross-border bus drivers and two customs officials provided key information, which was categorized and discussed along emerging themes. The women were mainly middle-aged single parents who engaged in ICBT for survival. On average, they were educated but forced into ICBT by economic hardships and lack of jobs associated with the closure of industries that started in the late 1990s. Deindustrialization, however, created opportunity for the women to obtain Zimbabwean passports and import clothes, blankets, electrical gadgets and vehicle spare parts from South Africa (SA). Hence, a delay in obtaining the passport which costs US$51 and issued within six months was the women's first challenge. Desperate to save meager incomes as most Zimbabweans resorted to ICBT, most of them slept in the open while in SA. Local authorities harassed them searching and confiscating undeclared goods. The women's children suffered as they missed their mothers' attention, control and love. Instead of helping the women's businesses flourish, government proposed banning imports to revive Zimbabwe's industrial sector.

Introduction

Women dominate the informal sector of 'developing' countries which include but are not limited to informal cross-border trade (ICBT). The Informal economy + cross-border trade (n.d.) defines cross-border trade as the buying and selling of goods and services between businesses in neighboring countries. The same dictionary defines an informal economy as a 'system of trade or economic exchange used outside state controlled or money based transactions.' It includes among other transactions street trading. Income generated by the informal economy is rarely recorded for taxation purposes and may be unavailable for inclusion in the calculation of the gross domestic product (GDP). Although its contribution is often unrecognized, the informal economy forms an integral component of Africa's economy with 60% of all trade being informal (Temkin, 2009).

Women in Sub-Saharan African (SSA) have a long history of involvement in informal trade that dates back to the colonial era particularly in the distribution of food and small consumer items as well as the trade of services (Portes & Haller, 2005). Women were involved in small-scale trade mainly because of the gendered construction of the colonial economy and society, which allowed only male access to formal education and employment (Marilyn, Martha, & Chen, 2001). Colonial laws and regulations further restricted women's access to urban areas and confined them to rural areas.

As a result, only a few women especially widows, divorcees or orphans who were accused of witchcraft or refused to marry unacceptable men found their way into urban economic life as 'beer brewers, fresh produce traders and hawkers and vendors' (Gaidzanwa, 1998). Gender discrimination in access to education and formal employment continued in some SSA countries in the post-colonial era, forcing women to join the informal trade sector. But, it is the adoption of economic liberalization under Structural Adjustment Programs (SAPs) that led to the growth of the informal sector and firmly placed women's position in informal trade (Tim, 2012). SAPs were introduced across Africa in the 1980s and 1990s with influence from the World Bank and International Monetary Fund (IMF).

SAPs led to many job losses as a result of the privatization of public enterprises. All this has forced the inhabitants of SSA countries including women to seek alternative livelihood strategies such as ICBT. Women became self-sustaining by looking inward to assist and cushion families against the effects of the SAPs (Marilyn et al., 2001). Cross-border trade equipped women with earnings and resources to contribute significantly to the upkeep of their households and at the same time empowered some of them with financial independence and control of their own resources (Tim, 2012). Across Africa, women represent 70–80% of the participants in ICBT involved in buying and selling of goods across national boundaries largely at a small scale (Bolivar & Omar, 2006).

In Southern Africa, widespread unemployment due to SAPs and the growing shortage of essential goods at home fostered a robust ICBT in countries like Zimbabwe, Zambia, Malawi and Mozambique. This trade, which is mainly legal, involves the import of small quantities of goods as the women informal traders do not qualify for bank loans but rely on meager family savings. They import not only goods and commodities considered essential and scarce in their countries but which would sell and bring money quickly (Portes & Haller, 2005). Some of these women are efficient in utilizing transport fares, accommodation fees and other expenditure as they trade in both directions (Gaidzanwa, 1998). In other words, they would take goods and commodities in demand in the host country for example South Africa (SA) and bring back goods in demand at home in Zimbabwe, Zambia, or one of the other countries in Southern Africa.

In Zimbabwe, the Economic Structural Adjustment Program (ESAP) that was implemented between 1991 and 1995 led to 'de-industrialisation, growing unemployment and the severe erosion of living standards of the majority' (Mlambo & Raftopoulos, 2010, p. 2). The downsizing and closure of some companies that started with ESAP continued as well as worsened in the 2000s due to a multidimensional crisis sparked by a series of disputed elections, the much-criticized 'fast track' land reform program, and violence against the opposition.

This raised further the rate of unemployment, reduced the purchasing power of the majority, and helped increase poverty to unprecedented levels. Unemployment that started with ESAP in the 1990s worsened in the 2000s. The closure of manufacturing industries further drove unemployment levels up (Murisa, 2010). This led to four among every five people being unemployed (Mashingaidze, 2006, p. 62). There was a decline in formal employment in urban areas from 3.6 million in 2003 to 480,000 in 2008 (Murisa, 2010, p. 5). The few who remained in formal employment earned wages below the poverty datum line as their incomes were 'eroded by the hyperinflationary environment' (Murisa, 2010, p. 5). All this put pressure on Zimbabwean women to join ICBT between home and economically stable countries in Southern Africa especially SA and Botswana in order to help families survive the economic crisis. The study informing this paper found out the challenges that these women face as well as the opportunity for the empowerment of these women and their families.

Generally, the dominance of women in the informal sector of developing countries reflects discrimination against their development in these societies which contributes to their disempowerment in several ways. For instance, a 2011 Bangladeshi poverty study noted that cultural norms, religious seclusion and illiteracy among women in many developing countries, along with a greater commitment to family responsibilities, prevent women from entering the formal sector (Colin & Windebank, 1998). When in the informal sector, the likelihood of ending up being poor is stronger for women than men since men have larger scale operations and deal in non-perishable items while there are few women employers who hire others (Gerald & Rauch, 2005). Instead, most women are involved in smaller scale operations and trade in food items, which fetch lower incomes, making a gendered income-gap wider in the informal than formal sector.

A few studies have shown the ability of ICBT to reduce poverty or empower women. Schneider (2002) and Colin (2005) started that ICBT is essential for poverty reduction. This is because an increase in women's incomes tends to collate with greater expenditure on children and family welfare, unlike similar increases in the incomes of men. Gerald and Rauch (2005) argued that ICBT provides specific opportunities for the empowerment of women through the development of informal and formal sector retail markets, the creation of employment opportunities to traders and their employees. With access to some capital, this creates an opportunity to alleviate poverty.

Despite their contribution to the national economies of their African countries, women's ICBT is not recognized and they do not grow due to the lack of access to credit, knowledge and technology (Tim, 2012). Instead of their ICBT being facilitated they are demonized (Gaidzanwa, 1998). For instance, women informal cross-border traders from other Southern African countries to SA are often harassed, subjected to xenophobic attacks and rounded up and deported by customs officials and the police especially in SA where they are less protected by law than at home (Gaidzanwa, 1998, Cross-border traders' experience, 2011). Their goods are often confiscated by these officials some of who demand bribes and/or sexual favors from these women in order to release them or their goods. This and other factors such as 'long periods of separation from family and friends may induce informal cross border traders to resort to casual sex ... to relive their boredom and loneliness' (Kurebwa, 2015, p. 67).

The women informal cross-border traders often lack knowledge about markets. For instance, informal traders involved in exporting maize from Northern Mozambique to

Southern Malawi were exposed to poverty by holding on to large stocks of maize due to a surplus maize production in Southern Malawi in 2003 (Temkin, 2009). Women cross-border traders also have lower literacy levels and are more likely to lack information and knowledge about cross-border trade regulations and procedures than their male counterparts (Gerald & Rauch, 2005). This results in their failure to benefit fully from the opportunities and efficiencies that border management reforms offer such as zero tax regimes. For instance, most women do not benefit from the Common Market for Eastern and Southern Africa (COMESA) trade regime which offers zero tax facilities (Schneider, 2002).

There are also challenges related to transportation whereby women cross-border traders spend lots of hours in transit or pay high costs to transport their goods. Although both men and women suffer from poor roads, the fact that women predominate among traders who use public transport means that they feel the implications of poor transport infrastructure more acutely (Gerald & Rauch, 2005). Village transport surveys in Tanzania and Zambia show that women spend nearly three times as much time in transport activities compared with men and transport about four times as much volume. Evidence from West Africa but with relevance to Southern Africa to indicate that road travel using public transport results in frequent delays, missed market days and goods becoming perishable (Roever, 2014; Tim, 2012). Women spend higher income shares on transportation cost than men, eroding their profits and reducing their ability to invest in businesses and other productive activities while trapping them in a vicious cycle of poverty (Babinard & Scott, 2009).

Women cross-border traders in Burundi felt that their government was uncooperative and oppressive as it failed to reduce border tariffs. They also felt bad about lacking information, which in turn made some of them afraid to take loans (Masinjila, 2009). Colin and Windebank (1998) argued that small traders face highly regressive costs but they have little choice except to trade informally. Moving to formal trade which requires them to register a company as well as for tax collection would attract more than double the border costs that they currently face as informal traders and would therefore force them out of business.

Since they have no other alternative but to trade informally, women cross-border traders have devised ways to cope with their challenges. Those studied by Muzvidziwa (2006) in Masvingo, Zimbabwe, had developed a positive view about their trade despite the challenges they faced. They were assertive, independent and goal oriented in their thinking and attributed their suffering to external forces beyond their control. They saw themselves as hard-working persons aimed at supporting their households such that if they failed to do so, disasters would be experienced. Women cross-border traders in Nigeria viewed constraints as inherently part of the cross-border trade. They viewed excessive harassment, exactions and very high customs duty as hard luck and they hoped to be able to recoup the losses on subsequent trips. At the same time, they resented the attitude of some officials and had hard feelings about them (Tim, 2012).

Objectives of the study

The study assessed the challenges faced by women ICBTs in the city of Mutare during a prolonged economic crisis in Zimbabwe. The specific objectives of the study on which this paper is based included to: (1) assess the characteristics of women involved in ICBT in the city of Mutare and the types of goods they sell; (2) analyze the opportunities and

challenges faced by the women involved in ICBT in the city of Mutare and (3) suggest solutions to these challenges.

Research methodology

The study adopted a qualitative paradigm in generating information. According to Creswell (2007) a qualitative study is defined as an inquiry process of understanding social
or human problems, based on building a complex, holistic picture, formed with words,
reporting detailed view of informants and conducted in a natural setting. A qualitative
approach was appropriate for this study since its aim was understanding in-depth and hol-
istically the challenges women cross-border traders face and doing justice to the complex-
ities of their social lives. Through this approach, the researcher had an insider's view of the
actors' own definitions. This allowed for 'a thick description' of the phenomenon under
study (Borg & Gall, 1996).

The study used in-depth interviews and key informant interviews for generating information. The population from which the sample was selected involved about 150 women
cross-border traders who sell their merchandise including clothing, electronics and shoes
imported mainly from SA at the Meikles Park Flea Market (MPFM). It also included about 20
drivers from 5 major bus companies plying the route between Mutare in Zimbabwe and
Johannesburg in SA and about 30 customs officials based at the Mutare branch of the Zimbabwe Revenue Authority (ZIMRA).

The study informing this paper was conducted at the MPFM which is found in the
central business district (CBD) of Mutare city. The city of Mutare is located in the
eastern highlands of Zimbabwe on the border with Mozambique. It is the fourth largest
city in Zimbabwe (Manyanhaire, Murenje, Chibisa, Munasirei, & Svotwa, 2007). The population of Mutare during the most recent census conducted in 2012 stood at 187,621 people
(ZimStat, 2013). The industrial base of Mutare like the other Zimbabwean cities was
severely diminished during the crisis between 2000 and 2008. As a result, 'unemployment
has sky-rocketed in Mutare like in the rest of Zimbabwe's urban centres. Consequently
most of the city's residents try to make a living through vending and other informal
sector activities' (Manyanhaire et al., 2007, p. 174).

From these total populations, 16 women informal cross-border traders were purposively selected out of 150 women selling their imported goods at MPFM. Two customs officials were also purposively selected out of about 30 based in Mutare and 2 cross-border
bus drivers out of about 20 plying the Mutare–Johannesburg route. In all cases, the
sample size was more than 5% of the total population size and therefore representative
of the total population according to the rule of thumb used by statisticians.

Purposive sampling was used to select the participants since they possessed rich information and experiences related to the challenges faced by women informal cross-border
traders in the city of Mutare. In purposive sampling, the researchers deliberately or in a
targeted way selected a sample that would effectively inform the research questions
guiding this study (Punch, 2009).

For a descriptive qualitative study like this one, the interview was the most appropriate
data generation tool. Interviews are a very reliable way of accessing people's perceptions,
meanings, and definitions of situations and their constructions of reality (Marshall &
Rossman, 2006; Punch, 2009). Interviews provide the interviewer with the chance to

respond immediately with follow-up questions to what the participants would have said (Punch, 2009). The researcher also has the opportunity to record non-verbal communication language, such as facial expressions or gestures which are all data. To understand these unspoken words, the researchers used a standard follow-up question: *I saw you acting in this way; may I know what meaning is attached to that gesture, facial expression or language?*

The three researchers sought the participants' informed consent before conducting the study in line with recommended ethical considerations. Participation was also voluntary following the signing of a consent form. Effort was made not to interfere with the smooth operation of the women's daily activities and they were assured of anonymity through the use of pseudo names.

Data analysis involved seven phases as suggested by Marshall and Rossman (2006) including: organizing the data, immersion in the data, generating categories and themes, coding the data, offering interpretations, and writing the report. Organization of data involved the researchers logging data according to dates, names, and times and when and with whom they were gathered. During immersion in the data, the researchers read, reread and read through the data once more so that they became intimately familiar with the data (Punch, 2009; Rudestam & Newton, 2007). Some of the data gathered using interviews was presented verbatim while the other was presented in tables before being described. Items that strongly addressed the same sub-problem were aggregated.

Results

Participants' socio-demographic data

Age distribution of the 16 women indicated that 7 of them, the majority, were aged 41–50 years (Table 1). Their second majority (5 out of 16) was aged 31–40 years old. Both the cross-border bus drivers and the customs officials were males. While the 2 cross-border bus drivers were in the 31–40 age range, both customs officials were aged 41–50 years old. None of the selected stakeholders in the cross-border trade business in Mutare was aged 51–60 years. This suggested that the cross-border business was for middle-aged women who have children and in some cases unemployed husbands to support. At these ages, these women probably had school-going children who needed constant supervision with schoolwork. Yet, this trade required these women to travel frequently outside the country to order new goods.

Seven out of the 16 women were still single while 6 were widows. Only 3 of the women were married. Among the married women, one of them belonged to a polygamous marriage. She joined cross-border trade because:

Table 1. Age and marital status of the women.

Age (years)	No.
Less than 30	4
31–40	5
41–50	7
Marital status	
Single	7
Widowed	6
Married	3

Source: Study findings.

Being the first wife among the 3 wives of Mandizvidza (pseudo name), my husband seemed to favour the other 2 wives probably because they are both employed. Therefore, I decided to join other women in the informal cross-border trade in order to boost the little I was given by my husband since the policy in the family is that a mother should nurture her own children.

This indicated that some of the women were pushed into ICBT by the need to provide for families single-handedly not only because they are widows but also due to some men who are lazy to work and support families. These findings particularly the high proportion of widowed women among the sample was consistent with previous studies. For instance, Gaidzanwa (1998) found that women in difficult circumstances including widows were among those who often joined ICBT.

Table 2 shows that half of the women cross-border traders had attained the Ordinary Level (or Form Four) while only four did not complete secondary school but dropped out after attaining Form Two. Most of these women had average education by Zimbabwean standards since passing Form Four is the minimum requirement for entry in both vocational training colleges and some formal jobs. This finding was contrary to the arguments made by other researchers that most women dominate the informal sector because they are less educated than men. Some of these women might have possessed the required passes at Form Four to join vocational training colleges or some jobs, but they failed to do so due to general lack of jobs and high unemployment levels that reach above 80% in Zimbabwe. Although others completed Form Four, they might not have possessed the required passes.

Regarding their occupations, the majority (12 out of 16) of these women were self-employed in the ICBT. This indicated that most of these women used ICBT for helping families survive during the prolonged economic crisis in Zimbabwe. On the other hand, one-quarter of the studied women combined ICBT with formal employment as teachers probably to supplement inadequate civil servant salaries. Civil servants particularly teachers who are diploma holders currently earn about US$500 per month, which might be inadequate for food and non-food needs of a family of six. This explains some of these teachers' need to supplement their salaries.

All the women had 6–10 years of experience as informal cross-border traders (result not shown). This suggested that most of them joined this trade in the mid-2000s when the crisis in Zimbabwe reached its peak. In other words, they were pushed into ICBT by economic hardships. This has a bearing on the women's attitudes towards any challenges faced since they have limited or no other alternatives but to operate informally.

On the other hand, the two drivers had four years of driving the women through international borders each and the customs officials had between six and seven years of working for the Zimbabwe Revenue Authority (ZIMRA). With this level of experience

Table 2. Education and occupation of the women.

Educational level of the women	No.
Diploma	4
Ordinary Level (Form Four)	8
Form Two	4
Occupation of the women	
Self-reliant	12
Teacher	4

Source: Study findings.

in ICBT, the key informants just like the women were knowledgeable in a number of issues regarding the business including the challenges that women cross-border traders face.

Goods bought and sold

Most of the women cross-border traders (11 out of 16) bring textiles, electrical gadgets and foodstuffs mainly from SA for resale in Mutare. Two out of 16 women sold spare parts for Japanese assembled vehicles. The closure or relocation of industries from Zimbabwe that started during ESAP created an opportunity for the women informal cross-border traders to sell almost everything including goods that fetch more money such as electrical gadgets and motor vehicle spare parts. This opportunity for the women has been necessitated by the fact that most Zimbabweans drive Japanese second-hand vehicles which are cheaper than the few that remain assembled locally or in nearby SA. This was stated by one of the women: *Zimbabweans only buy Japanese cars, but then, the unavailability of spare parts created an opportunity for us to supply the spare parts of such models.*

Three of the women were not specific about the goods they order from SA for resale in Zimbabwe. They simply said they buy from SA any goods that are on demand among local retailers in Mutare who are mainly Indians. The four women who were also teachers were not the only ones supplementing inadequate salaries but also the two drivers. One of the drivers said he supplied the local retailers with blankets, jeans and vehicle spare parts in order to supplement his cross-border driver's salary. The goods brought from SA for resale in Mutare by both the women and drivers were confirmed by the two customs officials as including piles of blankets, textiles (clothing), shoes, building materials and electrical gargets.

One of the customs officer commented:

> Ah! It's just unbelievable that women carry such bulky goods on a single bus trip. You really feel sorry for them when you request them to unpack the language in order to verify whether they have paid duty on their goods.

This is mainly because of the high demand for basic commodities in Zimbabwe such as blankets and clothes as a result of the closure of industries such as David Whitehead and Julie Whyte which used to produce such goods.

Challenges faced by the women when participating in ICBT

The women mentioned facing challenges where they order the goods in SA, on transit especially in SA, at the border when declaring or waiting to declare their goods, and in their homes when they are away in SA. While some of them do their shopping at the border town of Messina other travel further to central Johannesburg. In both cases, most of the women reported sleeping in the open either at the Beitbridge border post (SA side) or at Park Station where they get busses to Zimbabwe while in Johannesburg. This was confirmed by one of the women, Alleta Muchaneta (pseudo name), aged 39 years and from Chikanga high density suburb in Mutare when she recounted her recent trip to SA:

I was in South Africa for 2 days to buy goods for resale back in Mutare. I leave the comfort of my six-roomed fully furnished house to suffer the hardships of sleeping in an open space in a desperate bid to make a living.

This indicated that although Muchaneta has made it in life by owning a six-roomed house, she and her family still need to meet their food and other needs which they are able to get through her ICBT business. Another woman, Pauline Mhaka, is a widow who looks after three children alone. She joined informal cross-border trading after losing her formal job almost 10 years ago. Since, then, she has been traveling to various countries in the Southern African Development Community (SADC) region buying goods for resale back home. Mrs Mhaka said she had lost count of the number of times she has slept in the open including at Park Station in central Johannesburg since the income she gets from informal trading cannot afford her decent accommodation in the host countries.

I sleep at Park Station almost 4 times in two months. I have no money to book in a lodge or hotel, so this is the most appropriate place for me to sleep before I board a bus back home. We are harassed at the borders, at this place and even when we try to buy bulky commodities. We are treated like wild animals, our rights are seriously violated but we endure such situations because there is virtually nothing we can do.

There are several hundreds of other Zimbabwean women like Muchaneta who sleep in the open in the host country (SA) because the incomes they earn from ICBT are inadequate to pay for decent accommodation, which some of them might consider as a luxury. As a result, they endure sleeping in the open in foreign countries such as SA in order to save money to meet other needs in their lives. These women prefer buying the goods they sell at home in countries such as SA because they are cheaper than at home and there is the opportunity to trade in both countries as argued by Gaidzanwa (1998). Zimbabwean women often sell handcrafts in SA and use the money to buy food and other commodities that are in demand at home. As a result, a night in a cheap lodge or hotel in SA might be a luxury to these women whose main concern is survival.

By sleeping in the open, these women put themselves at risk of being robbed, raped or killed given the high prevalence of violence in SA. Some of them actually confessed that the next day they would be tired and irritable partly due to having uncomfortable sleep and failure to take a bath in the morning since such facilities are often unavailable at the bus station or border post where they sleep.

Another widow who looks after five children, Marvellous Ndoro, mentioned other challenges that the women informal cross-border traders face besides sleeping in the open in countries such as SA when buying goods for resale at home.

… Ill-treatment by authorities, uncomfortable sleeping, and lack of bathing. I am in this business not by choice but due to circumstances. The challenges I have endured range from obtaining the passport document, which takes several months to be issued, to harassment by customs officials and the police in South Africa. These officials are very unreceptive and have negative attitudes towards us (she was crying). Really, we operate under bad conditions.

This interview with Marvellous Ndoro helped identify two other challenges that are, obtaining the Zimbabwean passport and harassment by customs and police officials especially those in the host country (SA). Regarding the first challenge, the Zimbabwean passport like any other goods that were imported or used imported materials was difficult to obtain before 2009 and use of the hyperinflationary Zimbabwean dollar. Some people parted with as much as US$300 in order to obtain it sometimes through unofficial routes.

All this changed with the official adoption of multiple currencies dominated by the US dollar in February 2009. Since then, the ordinary Zimbabwean passport costs US$51 but takes up to six months to be issued. Those who need it within a short space of time such as two weeks should be prepared to part with US$250. Nevertheless, the ordinary Zimbabwean passport is still out of reach of the poorest people such as women who are single parents or those whose husbands are unemployed. This explains why some Zimbabweans looking for jobs still enter SA clandestinely although they do not require a visa but only the Zimbabwean passport which costs US$51. Due to their high frequency of traversing the distance between Zimbabwe and SA in order to replenish their goods, women informal cross-border traders usually cross the border legally using the Zimbabwean passport. This explains why a delay in being issued with the passport was a challenge for some of the women who desperately needed the passport in order to start or resume ICBT for survival.

Regarding the second challenge mentioned by Marvellous Ndoro, reports in Zimbabwean media confirmed that the women informal cross-border traders are often harassed by customs and police officials especially those in the host country (SA). This challenge becomes difficult to address since these women are often abused by authorities while in foreign lands and outside the jurisdiction of Zimbabwean authorities (Cross-border traders' experience, 2011). Similar challenges have been reported by other African women engaged in cross-border trade with their neighboring countries (Marilyn et al., 2001).

Another challenge reported by all the studied women was lack of enough time with their children including giving them adequate love. This resulted in some children being vulnerable to abuses of all kinds or being spoiled children. The situation was worse in the case of one of the married women who belonged to a polygamous marriage. She lamented that her children were caught in the crossfire of verbal or physical abuses inherent among the several wives in such marriages. Other studies found that females who are single parents face challenges in the administration of financial resources and assumption of new roles and responsibilities when they join ICBT (Temkin, 2009). Some of them mentioned in no uncertain terms that they have less time to help their children with homework and they are inconsistent in administering parental control and discipline. One of the studied women had this to say:

> Sorrowfully, my children feel less protected economically, have low self-esteem, are emotionally stressed and experience loss of identity along with a feeling that they have been neglected by their parent.

Figure 1 summarizes the women's other challenges. Harassment by customs officials and the police especially in the host country (SA) and stiff competition when selling the goods brought from SA were the challenges mentioned by all the women. Harassment involved the authorities searching and confiscating undeclared goods or those without valid passports. Some of the authorities demanded sexual favors in exchange for the release of the women or their goods as mentioned by one of the women. Some of the women confessed to bribing the officials or indulging in sex with them in order for them or their goods to be

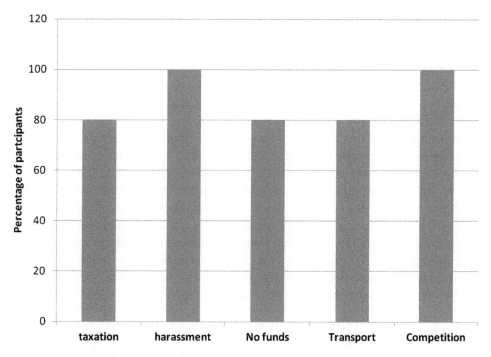

Figure 1. Other challenges faced by women informal cross-border traders in Mutare. Source: Study findings.

released. This exposed some of them to infection with sexually transmitted illnesses (STIs) such as HIV and AIDS. One of them had this to say:

> When my husband passed away, both of us were HIV negative. Oh-God! (face downcast). All this should have changed one day when I requested a haulage truck driver to assist me with money to pay off the excessive duty I was charged on my goods in exchange of sexual favours. I tell you my sister that was the night I suspect I got HIV infected, 'pafunge mwana wamai' (*think about the situations we face my sister*).

All this concurred with the findings by Gaidzanwa (1998) that instead of being facilitated, women cross-border traders are instead demonized, stigmatized, subjected to xenophobia attacks and often rounded up and deported. All the women concurred that the business was unhealthy physically, socially, emotionally and even spiritually. This is because it involves long hours of traveling on the bus from Mutare to Johannesburg in SA (about 1200 km) with sleepless nights and no chance to take a bath for 2–3 days. The situation is worse when one is having a period (menstruating) in which case one has to dispose of spoiled pads only without bathing. This supports other studies which have argued that more women than men face the negative health implications of informal cross-border trading and that the contours of HIV and AIDS transmission are evident at border crossings where customs procedures are slow and lack transparency (Marilyn et al., 2001).

The women cross-border traders also faced stiff competition from other Zimbabweans in the same trade since about 85% of Zimbabweans (Beitbridge burns: Zimbabweans protest against import ban, burn warehouse, 2016) have turned to the informal sector

since the closure of many industries in the country under complaints of viability challenges. Lack of funds to boost their businesses, having to pay duties and taxes at the
border and facing heavy penalties or the confiscation of goods if found defaulting as
well as transport costs were the other challenges mentioned by 80% of the women
cross-border traders each. Although mentioned by the second majority of these
women, the role played by these other challenges in the women informal cross-border
traders' businesses cannot be downplayed.

The customs officials confirmed that some of the women failed to access relevant information on duties and taxes charged at the border. As a result, they were subjected to
exploitative relations with intermediaries who often distort information. The customs officials also indicated that some of the women cross-border traders were unable to complete
import declaration forms especially those with lower levels of education. Others were
afraid of the consequences that they ignorantly thought they would face if they filled
the declaration forms. This was consistent with other studies which found that as a
result of low levels of literacy and lack of information and knowledge about cross-
border trade regulations and procedures, most women cross-border traders could not
fully benefit from border management reforms (Engqvist & Lantz, 2009; Marilyn et al.,
2001).

Solution to the challenges faced by women informal cross-border traders

The two customs officials concurred that the contribution of informal cross-border traders
to trade expansion and economic growth in Zimbabwe is undocumented/unrecorded and
as a result cannot be 'visible' to government officials and decision-makers. Other studies
found that despite the evident contributions of ICBT to national economies, mainstream
trade policies and institutions tend to neglect them (Marilyn et al., 2001).

When the researchers probed further, one of the customs officials said:

> The implication of ignoring this segment of the trading population is significant and it means
> that policy decisions are being made in response to incomplete data or information and that
> informal businesses may be not offered the support they need to expand.

Although all the women informal cross-border traders mentioned having unpleasant
relationships with the border officials, they could not do anything about this. They had
no alternative but to persevere through the challenges they face in this business in
order to continue feeding, educating and providing good health and decent accommodation for families. One of these women said, 'Ndodini, ndini mai, ndini baba, ndini tete,
ndini mbuya' (What else can I do, I am the mother, father, aunt and the grandmother of
my family). Instead, she prayed to God for good health and long life so that she continues
to provide for her family as a widow or single parent.

Instead of solving the women's challenges, the government of Zimbabwe proposed to
ban some of the goods imported by these women from SA for resale in Zimbabwe in order
to revive the countries industrial sector including building materials and household furni-
ture (Beitbridge burns: Zimbabweans protest against import ban, burn warehouse, 2016).
This resulted in violent protests from the ordinary Zimbabweans most of who survive on
cross-border trade between Zimbabwe and SA. This seemed to work since the government has not yet proceeded with this ban. If it were to happen, this would make the

women informal cross-border traders and their families plunge into deeper poverty. Studies conducted in Burundi found that women cross-border traders felt that their government was uncooperative and oppressive as it failed to reduce border tariffs (Masinjila, 2009).

Conclusion

Most of the women were middle-aged and single parents who engaged in ICBT for survival. On average, they were educated but forced into ICBT by economic hardships and lack of jobs caused by closure of many industries under an economic crisis that started during the ESAP (1991–1995) and worsened in the 2000s. The same company closures created opportunities for these women to sell basic commodities like clothing, blankets and goods that fetch more money such as electrical gadgets and motor vehicle spare parts. Most of the women sold handicrafts in SA and bought cheaper goods for resale in Zimbabwe. They used their Zimbabwean passports when crossing the border. This made a delay in obtaining the passport, which costs US$51 and takes up to six months, their first challenge. Desperate to save money for more basic needs, most of them slept in the open at the Beitbridge border post or a bus station in Johannesburg during trips to SA.

While in SA, most of them reported harassment (including searching and confiscating undeclared goods) by local authorities. Some of these authorities demanded sexual favors from the women in order to release them or their goods. The women also faced stiff competition from other traders given that most Zimbabweans have turned to ICBT for survival. Some of them wished they could access capital to boost the business. Back home, their children suffered as they missed their attention, control and love. This led all the women to concur that the business was unhealthy physically, socially, emotionally and spiritually.

The women endured all these challenges while their 'voices' were unheard by the government. The customs officials said since ICBT was undocumented, it remained 'invisible' to government officials and policy-makers. They also said some women relied on third parties for information on duty free arrangements. Others, especially those less educated, were unable to complete import declaration forms. Yet others were irrationally afraid of the consequences they thought would follow them after completing the forms. In either case, the women ended up having their undeclared goods confiscated by customs officials or the police and charged hefty fines. Some of them might have perceived this as the government charging them high duties or taxes.

The government has done nothing to help the women. Instead, it proposed banning the goods imported by the women from SA with the intention of reviving the country's industrial sector. A protest by informal cross-border traders led government to suspend this proposition. The government should indefinitely suspend the import ban and create more conducive conditions for the women to conduct their ICBT.

Recommendations for policy and further research

- The government of Zimbabwe should shelve its heavily protested policy to ban the importation of certain goods from SA which form these women's core business.

- Instead, it should identify and support clear value chains in the informal cross-border trading business so that everyone is not doing the same thing.
- The government with aid from private partners should also avail affordable loans and train local women so that they can become competitive and expand their businesses.
- The women also need training on balancing their attention between business and social responsibilities.
- Issues of ICBT should be mainstreamed in trade policies, poverty reduction strategies, national development plans and budgets.
- Existing information on tariff exemptions and market opportunities should be repackaged in user-friendly formats and disseminated to women informal cross-border traders with a clear communication strategy and also targeting the illiterate.
- The governments of both Zimbabwe and SA should cooperate in reducing the harassment of innocent women seeking a living by corrupt customs and police officials.
- In the long term, economic development is necessary in Zimbabwe in order to reduce reliance by most Zimbabweans on ICBT.
- Further research is needed especially covering other towns and cities in Zimbabwe to find out the extent to which the challenges cited by the women are affecting all women informal cross-border traders. Research is also necessary to assess the extent to which protests such as those conducted in Beitbridge against the banning of imports are effective to influence the Zimbabwean government to have policies that support ICBT.

Disclosure statement

No potential conflict of interest was reported by the authors.

References

Babinard, J., & Scott, K. (2009, October 27–30). *What can existing surveys tell us about gender and transportation in developing countries?* Paper presented at the 4th International Conference on Women's Issues in Transportation, Irvine, CA.
Beitbridge burns: Zimbabweans protest against import ban, burn warehouse. (2016, July 1). *New Zimbabwe*. Retrieved August 11, 2016, from http://www.newzimbabwe.com/news-29996-Protests+Beitbridge+burns,+Zimra+razed/news.aspx
Bolivar, G., & Omar, E. (2006). *Informal economy: Is it a problem, a solution, or both? The perspective of the informal business*. North-western University School of Law and Economics Papers, the Berkeley Electronic Press.
Borg, W. R., & Gall, M. D. (1996). *Educational research an introduction*. New York: Pearson.
Colin, C. (2005). The undeclared sector, self-employment and public policy. *International Journal of Entrepreneurial Behavior & Research, 11*(4), 244–257.

Colin, C. W., & Windebank, J. (1998). *Informal employment in advanced economies: Implications for work and welfare*. London: Routledge.

Creswell, J. W. (2007). *Designing and conducting mixed methods research*. Thousand Oaks, CA: Sage.

Cross-border traders' experience. (2011, November 6). *The Herald*. Retrieved August 2, 2016, from http://www.herald.co.zw/cross-border-traders-experiences/

Engqvist, J. H., & Lantz, M. (2009). *Dharavi: Documenting informalities*. Delhi: Academic Foundation.

Gaidzanwa, R. B. (1998). Cross-border trade in Southern Africa: A gendered perspective. In L. Sachikonye (Ed.), *Labour migration in Southern Africa* (pp. 83–94). Harare: SAPES Trust.

Gerald, M., & Rauch, J. E. (2005). *Leading issues in economic development* (8th ed.). New York: Oxford University Press.

Informal economy + cross-border trade. (n.d). *Business Dictionary*. Retrieved October 20, 2016, from http://www.businessdictionary.com/definition/informal-economy.html

Kurebwa, J. (2015). The vulnerability of female cross border traders to HIV and AIDS in Zimbabwe: The case of Beitbridge border post. *Journal of Humanities and Social Science, 20*(3), 65–69.

Manyanhaire, O. I., Murenje, T., Chibisa, P., Munasirei, D., & Svotwa, E. (2007). Investigating gender dimensions in vending activities in the city of Mutare, Zimbabwe. *Journal of Sustainable Development in Africa, 9*(4), 169–186.

Marilyn, C., Martha, A., & Chen, K. (2001). *Globalization and the informal economy: How global trade and investment impact on the working poor*. Background paper commissioned by the ILO Task Force on the Informal Economy, Geneva.

Marshall, C., & Rossman, G. B. (2006). *Designing qualitative research* (4th ed.). London: Sage.

Mashingaidze, T. M. (2006). The Zimbabwean Entrapment: An analysis of the nexus between domestic and foreign policies in a collapsing militant state, 1990s–2006. *Alternatives, 5*(4), 57–76.

Masinjila, M. (2009). *Gender dimensions of cross-border trade in the East African community – Kenya/Uganda and Rwanda/Burundi border*. Economic Commission for Africa: African Trade Policy Centre Work in Progress 78. Retrieved August 10, 2016, from http://www1.uneca.org/Portals/atpc/CrossArticle/1/WorkinProgress/78.pdf

Mlambo, A., & Raftopoulos, B. (2010, April 8–11). *The regional dimensions of Zimbabwe's multi-layered crisis: An analysis*. Election processes, liberation movements and democratic change in Africa conference, Maputo. Retrieved August 15, 2016, from http://www.cmi.no/file/%3F1011

Murisa, T. (2010). *Social development in Zimbabwe*. Discussion paper prepared for the Development Foundation for Zimbabwe. Retrieved August 15, 2016, from http://www.dfzim.com/wp-content/downloads/Social_Development_in_Zimbabwe_by_Dr_T_Murisa.pdf

Muzvidziwa, V. N. (2006). Women without borders: Transborder movements as a coping and investment strategy. *Africanus Journal of Development Studies, 36*(2), 180–153.

Portes, A., & Haller, W. (2005). The informal economy. In N. Smelser & R. Swedberg (Eds.), *Handbook of economic sociology* (2nd ed., pp. 403–425). New York: Russell Sage Foundation.

Punch, K. F. (2009). *Introduction to research methods in education*. London: Sage.

Roever, S. (2014, April). *Informal economy monitoring study sector report: Street vendors*. Manchester: Women in Informal Employment Globalizing and Organizing (WIEGO).

Rudestam, K. E. & Newton, R. R. (2007). *Surviving your dissertation: A comprehensive guide to content and process* (2nd ed.). London: Sage.

Schneider, F. (2002). *Size and measurement of the informal economy in 110 Countries around the World*. Boston: Tynwad Ltd.

Temkin, B. (2009). Informal self-employment in developing countries: Entrepreneurship or survivalist strategy? Some implications for public policy. *Analyses of Social Issues and Public Policy, 9*(1), 135–156.

Tim, R. (2012, February 9). Tax breaks for hiring a cleaner could save middle class thousands. *The Telegraph*.

ZimStat. (2013). *Census 2012 provincial report*. Manicaland. Retrieved from http://www.zimstat.co.zw/dmdocumentss/Census/CensusResults2012/National_Report.pdf

Recognizing Indonesian fisherwomen's roles in fishery resource management: profile, policy, and strategy for economic empowerment

Athiqah Nur Alami and Sandy Nur Ikfal Raharjo

ABSTRACT

This study examines the role of fisherwomen in fishery resource management in Talaud Island District, North Sulawesi District, Indonesia. Several focus group discussions, interviews and questionnaires with fisherwomen and fishermen community as well as relevant stakeholders in Talaud Islands were conducted to collect data about the issue. The results of the research show that most of the fisherwomen in the particular area earn a living as collecting mussels, making and repairing nets, trading fish, and processing fish products. Trading and processing are the sub-sectors where women's roles are over-represented which are low-grade unskilled jobs. However, the paper argues that the contribution of women in the fisheries sector has not been adequately reflected in policies and not yet transformed into women's economic empowerment. The paper concludes that women's roles and contribution to fishery family welfare and national development must be recognized by relevant government agencies and accomodated in national and local policies. These roles also should be transformed to women's economic empowerment.

Introduction

Fishing activities, particularly in the primary sector, traditionally is still seen as a male domain (Choo, Barbara, Kyoko, Kusakabe, & Williams, 2008; Frocklin, Torre-Castro, Lindstrom, & Jiddawi, 2013; Williams, 2008). Fishermen are usually regarded as providers/ hunters/fishers in fisheries activities (Harper, Zeller, Hauzer, Pauly, & Sumaila, 2013, p. 56). An understanding of the traditional role of the man contributes to the idea. In fact, fisherwomen, including women who catch fish for a living and wives of fishermen who directly or indirectly relate to her husband's activities, have important roles and make significant contribution to the fisheries sector.

The role of women in the fisheries sector become important findings in number of studies (Harper et al., 2013; Weeratunge, Snyder, & Choo, 2010). There has been an increase in the number of Asian women involved in the fisheries sector. Harper et al. (2013, p. 58) noted that about 33% of the workforce in the field of rural aquaculture in

China are women, while they are about 42% and 80% in Indonesia and Vietnam. FAO data in 2014 also showed that 19% of all people who are directly involved in the fishery primary sector activities such as fishing and aquaculture are women. However, if the secondary sector of fisheries, especially in small-scale fisheries, is counted then almost half of its work-force are women (FAO, 2016, p. 5).

Fisherwomen are predominantly engaged in pre-harvest (Harper et al., 2013; Weera-tunge et al., 2010) and post-harvest (Bennett, 2005) sectors. Their roles are various, from handling fish, gleaning the reef, collecting of food, financing the fleet, repairing nets, to processing and marketing the catch (Harper et al., 2013, pp. 58–59). Fisherwomen in East Coastal India, for example, play an important role in retailing, auctioning, sorting, grading, curing and drying, prawn peeling and collection of seaweed apart from hand-braiding and repair of nets (Biswas & Rao, 2014, p. 298). Along with those roles, women also prepare food for their husband and taking care of their families' educational, health and dietary needs (Bennett, 2005, p. 451). These roles may challenge the long-held notion that fisheries are mostly a male domain (Weeratunge et al., 2010, p. 407). As men-tioned further by Weeratunge et al. that work in fisheries began to appear as women's area when roles such as gleaning, trading, processing and fish farming are taken into account (2010, p. 406). In fact, women outnumber men in processing and trading fish around the world (Weeratunge et al., 2010, p. 407). Although women's participation is dominant in marketing, they tend to work nearer their homes (Immanuel & Rao, 2009, p. 412).

As can be seen in her study on the role of fisherwomen in Pekalongan, Indonesia, Anna finds that fisherwomen play roles essentially on facilitating the fisheries activities of their husband and distributing fisheries product within the communities and the market (Anna, 2012). It also has been the case for fisherwomen in Talaud Island regency, North Sulawesi. As one of the districts where most of its territory is sea, Talaud Islands needs to make the fisheries sector as the backbone of the economy so it is not surprising that the majority of people work as fishermen. Although the fisheries sector is still perceived as male domain, women's roles as actors cannot be ignored. Fisherwoman in Talaud district mostly played a role in the secondary sectors such as fish processing and sales.

However, these roles are usually unrecognized and uncounted as productive activities (FAO, 2016; Williams, 2008; Williams, Hochet-Kibongui, & Nauen, 2005). As argued by Zhao, Tyzack, Anderson, and Onoakpovike (2013, p. 70), lack of recognition of women fisheries is an important issue of concern. Women's roles in near shore fishing is also undervalued and invisible in the fisheries value chain. The undervalued role of women in the management and the use of natural resources is described by Bennett (2005, p. 451) as a reflection of their gender hierarchies in society. In fact, the finding of Allison and Ellis (2001) shows that the contribution of fisherwomen in fish marketing to livelihoods of family is evident. Weeratunge et al. (2010, p. 406) argues that money earned by women in fisheries activities contributes to the local economy and in some areas fishermen used the money as capital to improve their productive assets.

Even though women appear to have an important role in the fisheries sector, they still face a number of constraints that can reduce their access to fisheries resources and assets. For instance, they are oftenly low-paid or unpaid with unofficial status (FAO, 2016, p. 33). Fisherwomen also still poor, as estimated that 70% of the world's poor are women (FAO, 2016, p. 134). Limitation of women's roles in the fishing value chain impacts on the dis-parity in their incomes, hence most of them are still poor. This poverty then brings consequences on the survival of not only women but also families. According to Weeratunge et al. (2010, p. 406), gender disparities affect the livelihoods of women and the entire household and community. This is a barrier to access to financial resources and policy support for these women. Moreover, since fishing is regarded as an activity with high level of uncertainty, fisherwomen can also be impacted on the uncertainty. As argued by Anna (2012, p. 145) fisherwomen face insecurity and risks in conducting their roles, not only in terms of environmental risks but also competition in fishery markets. These problems show that fisherwomen's significant roles have not correlated fully to their life improvement. Hence, there is a need to transform their significant roles to economic empowerment. For that reason, improving women's incomes, educational levels, access to information and ability to participate in decision-making processes may enhance the capabilities of the entire household and of society in general (Weeratunge et al., 2010, p. 406) as well as women's empowerment.

Various experiences have shown that using a gender lens in researching and formulating fisheries policy, including in relation to women's empowerment, become absolutely necessary. The problem, according to Williams (2008, p. 180) is that fisheries have long been weak on a gender perspective, focusing mainly on the fish stocks and fish production conducted predominantly by men. Williams et al. (2012, pp.1–2) also argue that women and gender is a topic 'not on the agenda' in aquaculture and fisheries. This issue are also missing from key global normative fisheries (and aquaculture) products such as the Code of Conduct for Responsible Fisheries (FAO, 1995) and other instruments and technical guidelines. The using of gender lens, according to Williams (2008, p. 180), provides a better and complete picture of the whole fishing industry and social context. Since the approach provides much more of the nature of fisheries, it becomes the basis for understanding the issues and suggesting more appropriate action. Also, the gender lens reinforces the importance of an integrated and complete supply chain approach to fisheries, a vital factor for a sector that produces a heavily traded commodity. Without the gender lens, fisheries and aquaculture studies and actions tends to value only fish production and fish stocks and the knowledge and roles directly linked to these.

In addition, although gender roles are important for the study of fishing communities, they are more often depicted in the study of anthropology and overlooked in the socioeconomic research. As a result, most studies in the fisheries have paid less attention to fisherwomen's contribution in the discourse. Bennett (2005, pp. 451–452) affirms that this is due to a number of factors. National policy agenda is still focused on the productive side or catching activity of fishery that is male-dominated. Hence, the processing and marketing that are dominated by women is underexplored. Women's work in nearshore activities goes unnoticed in fisheries studies and statistics which are dominated by attention to men's nearshore and offshore fishing (Weeratunge et al. 2010, p. 407). In the case of Indonesia, Fitriana and Stacey (2012, p. 160) outline that women in coastal villages are usually identified by the governments as fishermen's wives and their work is considered part of domestic work of caring for families and household. This classification means the work of women in fisheries is not counted in national government census collections under fisheries-related employment at district administrative level. Moreover, during the data collection activity in the field, researchers often do not include women in the process such as interviews or discussions. Consequently, the findings seem to gender-blind and fail to see the big picture of the fisher family. Another cause lies in the lack of disaggregated data, because the data on fisheries are part the agricultural sector. It creates the same situation for gender-based data.

Even if there have been a number of studies in fisheries policy, not many of them discuss the aspects of fisherwomen's economic empowerment. In spite of fisherwomen's roles, not enough attention has been given to targeting the focus of empowerment policies and programs at these enterprises which have greater potential at impacting women. In fact, the magnitude of fisherwomen's roles should have correlation to the women's economic empowerment so that women are more independent and able to escape from poverty. Lack of studies on women empowerment in fisheries is also acknowledged by Babalola, Bajimi, and Isitor (2015) in their study on the economic potentials of fish marketing and women empowerment in Nigeria. Babalola et al. (2015, p. 9929) finds that fish had huge marketing potential for the economic empowerment of the women if there are supported relevant policies. However, they acknowledge that there are still problems to be addressed such as the low education status of women that undermine their roles in marketing and lack of policies that can guarantee sale, price stability and improvement in the microfinance scheme. Lack of marketing skills and adequate training are also identified by Kanaga, Rajakumar, Sivasankar, Sruthi, and Gowsalya (2015, p. 219) as constraints for fisherwomen in running their business. Also, because the contribution of women is still poorly assessed, gender-aware policies have not been adequately formulated (FAO, 2016, p. 122).

In an attempt to fill this knowledge gap, the paper focuses on recognizing fisherwomen's roles in Talaud Islands and how their roles can be transformed to economic empowerment. This paper argues that economic empowerment is the condition or action where women gain opportunities and have autonomy in making decision to improve their economic life. According to Kabeer (1999), economic empowerment has an essential function on underpinning of wider social and political empowerment of women, both as individuals and as a collective marginalized groups. As mentioned by Harper et al. (2013, pp. 58–59), for example, the active participation of women in fishers' microfinance makes them self-reliant and economically empowered. The involvement of women in small-scale fisheries are also important, because as Hauzer et.al (2013, p. 28) suggest, this kind of fishery has the potential to contribute directly or indirectly to food security, livelihoods and economic security.

Therefore, there is a need to more clearly target and empower women throughout the value chain so that they have rights they can exercise on a sustainable basis. There should be a strategy for economic empowerment of fisherwomen because explicit empowerment of women can strengthen the fisheries value chain (FAO, 2016, p. 172). As an economic, social and political process, Pereznieto and Taylor (2014, p. 234) argue, empowerment should transform women's situation from a limited power condition to an enhanced power for the purpose of advancement. Drawn from this definition, they suggest that there are four areas of power where empowerment can bring about transformation on women's life. They are: *power within* the knowledge or individual capabilities; *power to* economic decision-making; *power over* access to and control over resources; and *power with* others to organize and enhance economic activity.

Hence, the paper argues that the aspect of economic empowerment of fisherwomen should be given more attention by any related stake holders. There is a need to create greater economic opportunities for fisherwomen in fishery sectors. This study attempts to contribute to the knowledge in the issue as well as informs policy-makers with evidence-based information. To discuss the issue, the study aims to analyze the roles of fisherwomen in the Talaud Islands, in terms of its profiles and policies. It also formulates strategies to transform these roles into economic empowerment.

Methodology

Study area

The research was undertaken in Talaud Islands in April 2012. Talaud Islands is a district in North Sulawesi Province which directly become Indonesia's maritime border area towards the Mindanao of the Philippines. Administratively, Talaud Islands consist of 19 subdistricts, in which the largest one is Beo Utara (144.85 km^2) located in Karakelang Island, while the smallest one is Miangas (2.39 km^2) that only consist of an island and its surrounding water (BPS, 2011). This district also has four foremost border islands: Miangas, Marampit, Intata and Kakorotan. While Miangas island become special subdistrict, the others belong to Nanusa subdistrict.

The territory consists of 96.8% waters, while the rest are some group of small islands (BPS, 2011). It has 17 islands scattered into 4 group of islands, namely Karakelang, Nanusa, Salibabu and Kabaruan (Dewi, 2015). Moreover, the district is also surrounded by Sulawesi Sea in the west and Pacific Ocean in the east. These position then lead to the condition that the livelihood of Talaud people is very related to and may depend on the sea (Figure 1).

The Talaud Islands are rich in fishery resources. It has 4008.94 ha of coral reefs area, comprised by fringing reef, patch reef and deep reef (DKP Kabupaten Kepulauan Talaud, 2012). The existence of the reefs is crucial for the fish reproduction process as well as habitat for some kinds of fish. In the Talaud Islands and its surrounding waters,

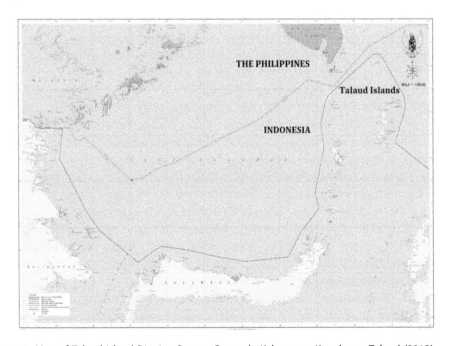

Figure 1. Map of Talaud Island District. Source: Bappeda Kabupaten Kepulauan Talaud (2012).

there are three dominating types of fishery resources: small pelagic, large pelagic and demersal. Small pelagics are fish species whose habitat is located at a depth of 0–200 m, such as tunny, *layang*, flying fish, mackerel and anchovies. Large pelagics are fish species whose habitat is located at a depth of over 200 m, namely tuna, skipjack, yellowfin, voyage, mackerel and shark. Meanwhile, demersal fishes are species that live at the bottom of the sea such as pomfret, grouper, red snapper and yellow tail (Mallawa, 2006). From a total of 333,600 tonnes capture fisheries annually, small pelagic shares 69.21%, large pelagic contributes to 21.01%, while demersal accounts for 7.4% (Ministry of Marine Affairs and Fisheries, 2011).

Regarding to the rich resources above, the fishery is inevitably part of the livelihood of people in Talaud Islands. There are 83,434 people live in Talaud districts in 2010, consisting of 51.14% male and 48.86% female. In all, 36.76% of the population work in the fishing sector (BPS, 2011). They not only made up of fishermen, but also fisherwomen. While fishermen play an important role in catching fish at the sea, fisherwomen play a significant role in the processing and marketing activities. However, the fisheries sector accounted for only 5.68% to the Talaud's GDP (BPS, 2011). Meanwhile, the number of poor households is still high, that is, 43% from the total 25,253 households (BPS, 2011). It shows that the wealth of the fisheries resources has not yet positively contributed to the welfare of Talaud people.

Data collection

Two types of data are used in this study. First is the primary data as collected by interviews, focus group discussions, questionnaires and observations. Interviews were held with 10 fisherwomen (age 20–50) and 10 fishermen (age 50–60) at 4 different fishing community around the district: Melonguane, Salibabu, Beo and Miangas. The sites were selected based on information from local governments, to cover different characters of fishing community in different locations. The interview is guided by several questions on traded species, markets, customer and perceptions on gender relations. Focus group discussions were also conducted among fishing community which is divided by fishermen community and fisherwomen community. The discussions cover some issues and clarify findings during the interviews. The data were also derived from a review of literatures that provide background on the role and contribution of women in the fisheries sector, which saw a wide range of experience in a number of countries.

Data analysis

The respondents' answers were organized, transcribed and categorized based on their pattern. The data were analyzed according to the gender analysis framework or Harvard framework to provide a comprehensive picture of gender relations in fishery sector in Talaud. Those data were used to identify and analyze the profiles of fishermen and fisherwomen in terms of activity, access and control in managing fishery resources. Regarding to the profiles, analysis on the implementation of the government's fishery policies in central and local level was conducted, followed by the formulation of the suggested strategy for fisherwomen's economic empowerment.

Results and discussion

Profiling fisherwomen's roles in Talaud Islands

This part attempts to map the profile of fishermen and fisherwomen's roles in fishery sectors in Talaud Islands with Harvard Framework analysis techniques. It makes the categorization of the type of fishing which is determined by the type of fishing based on dominant tools and means of capture in the fishing community of Talaud Islands. They are the fishing boat without an engine (rowing/canoe), boat engine (*pamboat*) and fishermen divers (*Jubi*). Mapping pattern of gender relations of any kind of fishing is divided into three stages as part of efforts to see the stages of fishery management: pre-production (pre-fishing), the production process (fishing) and post-production (post-fishing). Each stage and profile that constitute gender relations are distinguished by gender which is male and female. This is done with the assumption that there are different pattern of relations between men and women in every stage of fishery management. It is also reflected on the differences in activity, access and control. The difference in this relationship pattern reflects the occurrence of gender inequality between men and women in the fishing family.

Mapping the activity profiles of men and women in the family fishing is the identification of the everyday activities related to the management of fishery resources. The profile of fishery resources management indicates that the pattern of activities performed by men and women in the fishing family. This daily activity is not conducted in the same way because it is influenced by several factors such as the weather and the availability of fuel. These factors affect the fishery resources management ranging from fishing to selling the catch.

Generally, in Table 1, it can be seen that men and women in fishing family have roles in every stage of the fishery resources management. There is no significant differences in the roles and it is directly visible from all three types of fishing. Men and women in the fishing family in the three types of fishing not only play a productive role, which is directly related to the economic dimension of fishery resource management. They also perform domestic and social roles, which is generally not considered to be economic value but be a supporting factor in the series of fishery resource management. However, these roles do not spread evenly between men and women. There is a dominant roles played by one group, whether male or female, as well as the roles played by both. Besides, these roles do not always correlate with the access and control of resources.

At the pre-production stage, for example, fishermen and fisherwomen in all three types contribute to play a productive role in fishery resource management. Fishermen are usually in charge of preparing various fishing tools and means to go to sea, while the fisherwomen prepares supplies to be brought by the husband. For non-engine fishermen, they have to prepare a boat/canoe, paddle, hook, fishing line, as well as a longline fishing gear (for fishermen with machine boat). They prepare these tools of fishing early in the morning before going to sea, while the *Jubi* fishermen set them up in the afternoon. This activity indicates men and women have access to each resource associated with their roles. However, they have different controls for each type of resource. Also, husband and wife in a fishing family do not play the same domestic role. Along with setting up the husband's fishing needs, the wives also take care of the needs of other family members,

Table 1. Profile of men and women daily activities in fishermen's households.

Activities	Person	
	Men	Women
Productive roles		
Check the sea and the weather conditions	V	
Prepare fuel	V	
Prepare the means of capture	V	
Prepare the fishing gear	V	
Heading seaward	V	
Prepare the pond (aquaculture)		V
Spread fingerlings (aquaculture)		V
Feed (aquaculture)	V	V
Sell the captured fish	V	V
Make salted fish		
Chop the fish	V	
Clean the fish		V
Look for salt		V
Salt the fish		V
Dry the salted fish		V
Sell the salted fish	V	
Make smoked fish		
Chop the fish	V	
Clean the fish		V
Look for wood	V	
Clamp the fish with wood sticks		V
Make live coals		V
Grill the fish		V
Dry the fish	V	
Sell the smoke fish	V	V
Make fish crackers		
Clean and skin the fish		V
Make the fish dough		V
Boil the fish dough		V
Dry		V
Sell fish crackers		V
Dry sea cucumbers		
Clean sea cucumbers		V
Boil sea cucumbers		V
Grill sea cucumbers		V
Dry sea cucumbers	V	V
Sell sea cucumbers	V	V
Farm	V	V
Work as government employees	V	V
Open a stall at home		V
Make ice cubes		V
Domestic roles		
Prepare food to bring to sea		V
Escort to the beach		V
Carry fishing equipment		V
Prepare food and drinks		V
Set fire to warm the body		V
Fetch water for daily use		V
Cook		V
Do laundry		V
Prepare children for school		V
Take children to school		V
Parenthood	V	V
Social roles		
Worship	V	V
Women activity		V
Regular social gathering		V
Project development activities	V	V
Community service	V	V

Source: Alami (2015).

especially their children. However, at the pre-production stage, boat fishermen and non-engine fishermen do not necessarily play social role, because they have to go to sea in the morning. This condition is somewhat different for diver fishermen, where they generally go to sea in the evening, so that they have time to play domestic and community roles in the morning until the afternoon.

In the production stage, fishermen dominate in playing their roles, so that they have access to and control of resources involved in the role. This shows that fisherwomen do not directly relate to productive roles in fishery resources management as well as in the access and control over related resources. Meanwhile, the wives of diver fishermen experience different conditions, as they usually play a role in finding sea cucumbers at the beach or when the condition of the sea is receding. Even so, when the husband is at sea, the wife usually goes to the garden to plant sweet potato/chili/vegetable, garden watering, weeding and cleaning gardens. Not all gardening activities indeed are produced for commercial reasons, but the crops can be used to meet family needs and maintain food security. In some situations, fishermen contribute to the social activities such as working together in development projects at the village. This pattern of roles division is applicable when the season is in good condition, which usually occurs in December to June each year. If the season was not good enough, the fishermen becomes a farmer and performs other social roles.

The final stage of fishery resources management is called post-production that typically includes sales and processing of the catch. In this stage, fishermen and fisherwomen in all three types play productive roles. At the processing stage, they have a division of labor based on their capabilities. In this stage, they have the same access and control of the fish catches to be processed. Usually, fisherwomen do processing of the fish into salted fish, smoked fish and dried sea cucumber. In the process of salting and curing fish, for example, men have the task of splitting and cleaning fish, while the women are in charge of fish salting. This role generally played by non-engine fishermen and engine fishermen. While, the wife of diver fishermen are usually in charge of cleaning and boiling the sea cucumbers, and the husband has the task of drying them. There are different conditions in terms of selling activities. It has been the task of fisherwomen to sell the fish to the neighbors. In this activity, fisherwomen have access to and control over resources. They also have the power to determine the selling price of fish, of course by taking into account the costs incurred for the needs of fishing such as fuel. Furthermore, fisherwomen are also entitled to control the spending of money from the sale of fish.

These profiles show that fisherman and fisherwomen across different types of fisheries play roles in fishery activities. It is acknowledged that men is dominant in almost the entire chain of fisheries. It did show that the characteristics of the fishery still put these occupations as men's domain. Nevertheless, the role of fisherwomen also cannot be ignored. A total of 79.3% wives of fishermen earn a living as collecting mussels and in fish product processing or trading, and make or repair nets. Economically, they also contribute to the family income by opening a small shop at home and having a fishing industry at home. The problem, in the case of Talaud shows that, as mentioned by local administrative staff, a group of women are still marginalized and attract less attention. There is a lack of supporting socio-cultural environment for the advancement of women, which is rooted in the traditional view of culture and society. Hence, they still face marginalization in terms of their status, rights, roles and opportunities as well as less adequate acknowledgement in local and national policies.

Assessing fisherwomen's roles in policies

At the national level, the Indonesian government has enacted Act No. 31 of 2004 on Fisheries, which was then changed by Act No. 45 of 2009. These laws make up the waters of Indonesia as Fisheries Management Areas. According to the Regulation of the Minister of Marine Affairs and Fisheries No. 1 of 2009, Fisheries Management Area is a management area for fishing, aquaculture, conservation, research and development of fisheries covering the waters, the archipelagic waters, territorial sea, contiguous zone and exclusive economic zone of Indonesia. Fisheries Management Areas aim to achieve optimal management and sustainable fisheries and to ensure the sustainability of fish resources and the environment. The above rules divide Indonesian waters into 11 Fisheries Management Areas. Talaud Islands water was included in the Fisheries Management Area No. 716 that includes the Sulawesi Sea and the northern part of the Halmahera Island. In addition, the central government also set fishery as a key sector for the economic corridor of Sulawesi Island in The Masterplan for Acceleration and Expansion of Indonesia's Economic Development (MP3EI) 2011–2025 (Coordinating Ministry of Economic Affairs, 2011).

In local government level, Talaud Islands district has pointed out fishery sector as one of its priority in the Long-Term Regional Development Planning (RPJPD) 2005–2025. Fishery and agriculture is projected to be the main sector which contributes 34.24% of Talaud economy in 2025 (RPJPD Talaud, 2005, p. 204). In order to improve farmer and fisher capacities, they will develop farmer and fisher group, increase fisheries extension, as well as establish education and training center (RPJPD Talaud, 2005, p. 150). These programs are also related to policy on establishing Minapolitan development program in Lirung island, one of Islands in the district.

However, there are some constraints in the implementation of these policies. In national and local levels, there are still no aggregated data on Talaud fisherwomen. The term of 'nelayan' is merely defined as people who 'capture' fish for their livelihood (article 1, Act No. 45 of 2009). This definition seems to not acknowledge the role of people who live in fishery sectors but not in capturing activities, for example, processing the fish which most fisherwomen play in. Therefore, when there is a program for empowering 'nelayan', the government tend to only include fishermen who definitely capture fish, ignoring the fisherwomen behind.

This situation leads to the next problem which is the ignorance of fisherwomen's roles and competence in fishery sectors. Most of fisherwomen in Talaud play roles in fish processing and fish marketing, but still in traditional ways. They collect shells on the beach, sell extractive fish around to the neighbors, as well as process the fish into smoked fish by using limited equipments. However, there have been lack of policies on upgrading their skills on these activities and expanding marketing network to sell their fishery products. Fisherwomen also have roles in managing money in family, but they also have limited access to financial loans that may contribute to enhance their economic life.

The development of Minapolitan policy at Lirung islands, for example, also still focuses on the physical dimension which is men's domain, namely the provision of a collective boat (*pajeko*), cold storage usage and the establishment of fish port (Astuti, & Raharjo, 2015). *Pajeko* is used in the process of capturing fish by fishermen, while cold storage and fish port is intended to boost the sale process. Also, this policy implementation is more directed to the provision of facilities to capture fish. Government's fishery agency granted boat with *purse seine* (ring trawl, locally known as 'pukat cincin') to the certain fishermen groups. For women's empowerment, local governments actually has organized training on making fish balls and fish chips in some coastal villages close to the district's capital. However, the training could not be delivered intensively to the women in the foremost islands due to the lack of transportation services.

The absence of policies and programs for women may bring impacts not only to fisherwomen, but also to the fishermen and their households. They only can sell fresh fish in a cheaper price, which means less income for the households. In addition, when they cannot sell it quickly, the fish will decay and they have to throw it in vain to the sea. Therefore, there is a need to acknowledge the role of fishermen and fisherwomen in the regulation and empower them proportionally in policy implementation.

Transforming fisherwomen's roles into economic empowerment

The previous section noted that the fisheries sector in Talaud is still dominated by men and is supported by a fisheries policy that makes men policy targets. In fact, fisherwomen play roles in the value chain of fisheries that cannot be ignored, so it requires support at the policy level, especially in terms of economic empowerment. Drawing from Perezneito and Tylor, women's economic empowerment in this paper refers to efforts to transform women's situation from a limited power condition to four areas: an enhanced *power within* the knowledge or individual capabilities; *power to* economic decision-making; *power over* access to and control over resources; and *power with* others to organize and enhance economic activity (Perezneito & Taylor, 2014, p. 234). Therefore, based on the four dimensions of power that can make women more empowered, there are a number of efforts to transform the role of women into the real economic empowerment.

First, there should be efforts to enhance the power within their knowledge and individual capabilities. Since fisherwomen in the Talaud Islands have expertise on fish processing, there should be policies or programs to increase and upgrade their knowledge on this sector. It can function as value-added activities for fisherwomen to earn additional income for their family. In doing this program, the government may cooperate with business sector to optimize the outcomes. This effort will contribute positively to reduce poverty in the local society.

Secondly, fisherwomen should be empowered in economic decision-making among three levels: household, community and market. The Talaud Islands experience shows that fisherwomen play roles to determine the selling price of fresh fish. However, because most of them has less education, they do not have many knowledge and skills on financial management. Therefore, there should be policies that aim to enhance women's capacities in marketing to get economically empowered.

Thirdly, fisherwomen in the Talaud Islands should have power over access and control on financial, physical and knowledge-based asset in their family. In related to this, there should be policies to give financial loans to fisherwomen to expand their small business such as shops at home and support their entrepreneur initiatives. Another important thing is the need to deal with traditional and cultural barriers on accessing and controling those resources.

Lastly, in supporting fisherwomen's roles in fishery sector, there should be an institutional approach in policies, such as the establishment of fishery cooperatives. It is an effort to organize with others to enhance economic activity such as microfinance and their rights, including their price negotiating power with market. Through their involvement in this institution, fisherwomen can obtain benefits in gaining access to new markets and improving their ability to negotiate with fish suppliers. In the long term, this policy can strenghten the economic development and empowerment not only among fisherwomen but also local communities. Also, according to FAO (2009), cooperatives could improve the resilience and stability of fishing communities.

Conclusion

Fishery resources management has a strategic meaning for the improvement of Talaud Islands's welfare. To do so, fishermen and fisherwomen recently has set unwritten mechanism of such division of labor. Both parties play important roles which complement each other in productive, domestic and social activities. While fishermen tend to have full access and control over fishery production stage, fisherwomen have become prominent actors in post-production stage.

Unfortunately, those division of labor has not been recognized proportionally in the fishery policies and programs. Related governmental agencies tend to more focus on physical dimension of fishery that can be more easily found on the production stage. While the role of fisherwomen on non-physical dimension and non-directed activities are inadequately touched.

Since fishermen and fisherwomen roles are a series of complementary activities, the neglection on one part will disturb other parts. Therefore, the recent fishery resources management in Talaud seemed to be less optimal, especially as the efforts to elevate Talaud's people welfare.

Therefore, economic empowerment should be done, not only for fisherwomen, but also for fishermen. But since the previous policy implementation left the fisherwomen behind, such greater efforts should be conducted to set a balanced level of playing between the two genders. The strategy for economic empowerment of fisherwomen should cover some areas including individual capabilities, economic's decision-making, access and control on resources and organizing capabilities. To effectively implement these strategies, there should be a coordinated interagency cooperations from government, private and civil society actors by ensuring and enforcing gender mainstraiming strategy in the fishery resources management.

Acknowledgement

The authors would like to thank the Indonesian Institute of Sciences for funding the research entitled "Strategy of Border Area Development through Gender-based Natural Resource Management" from 2012–2014. They would also like to deliver appreciation to the team members and all informants who have shared information and documents, especially the government of Talaud Islands District, National Border Management Agency and BPS-Statistics Indonesia. The authors assume full responsibility for the content.

Disclosure statement

No potential conflict of interest was reported by the authors.

References

Act of the Republic of Indonesia Number 31 of 2004 on Fishery.
Act of the Republic of Indonesia Number 45 of 2009 on the change of the Act Number 31 of 2004 on Fishery.
Alami, A. N. (2015). The gender-based fishery resource management in fishermen's households in Natuna and Talaud Islands regencies. In A.N. Alami (Ed.), *Gender-based natural resource management in Indonesian marine borders* (pp. 87–126). Yogyakarta: Pintal.
Allison, E. H., & Ellis, F. (2001). The livelihoods approach and management of small-scale fisheries. *Marine Policy, 25*, 377–388.
Anna, Z. (2012). The role of fisherwomen in the face of fishing uncertainties on the North Coast of Java, Indonesia. *Asian Fisheries Science Special Issue, 25S*, 145–158.
Astuti, Y., & Raharjo, S. N. I. (2015). Fishery resource management in development policies in border areas in Natuna and Talaud Islands Regencies. In A. N. Alami (Ed.), *Gender-based natural resource management in Indonesian marine borders* (pp. 55–86). Yogyakarta: Pintal.
Babalola, A. D., Bajimi, O., & Isitor, S. U. (2015). Economic potentials of fish marketing and women empowerment in Nigeria: Evidence from Ogun State. *African Journal of Food Agriculture, Nutrition and Development, 15*(2), 9921–9934.
Bappeda Kabupaten Kepulauan Talaud. (2005). *RPJPD Kabupaten Kepulauan Talaud 2005–2025*. Melonguane: Bappeda Kabupaten Kepulauan Talaud.
Bappeda Kabupaten Kepulauan Talaud. (2012). *Kondisi Sosial Demografi Kabupaten Kepulauan Talaud*. A Presentation in Focus Group Discussion on April 3, 2012, Melonguane.
Bennett, E. (2005). Gender, fisheries and development. *Marine Policy, 29*, 451–459.
Biswas, M. P., & Rao, M. R. M. (2014). Fisherwomen of the East Coastal India: A study. *International Journal of Gender and Women's Studies, 2*(2), 297–308.
BPS. (2011). *Kabupaten Kepulauan Talaud dalam Angka 2011*. Melonguane: BPS Kabupaten Kepulauan Talaud.
Choo, P. S., Barbara, S., Kyoko, N., Kusakabe, & Williams, M. J. (2008). Guest editorial: Gender and fisheries. *Development, 51*, 176–179.
Coordinating Minsitry of Economic Affairs and National Development Planning Agency. (2011). *Masterplan percepatan dan perluasan pembangunan ekonomi Inonesia 2011–2025*. Jakarta: Coordinating Minsitry of Economic Affairs.
Dewi, R. (2015). The condition of marine borders in Natuna and Talaud Islands regencies. In A. N. Alami (Ed.), *Gender-based natural resource management in Indonesian marine borders* (pp. 33–54). Yogyakarta: Pintal.
DKP Kabupaten Kepulauan Talaud. (2012). *Kebijakan pengelolaan sumberdaya kelautan dan perikanan di pulau-pulau perbatasan di kabupaten Kepulauan Talaud*. A Presentation in Focus Group Discussion on April 3, 2012, Melonguane.
FAO. (1995). *Code of conduct for responsible fisheries*. Rome: Author.
FAO. (2009). *Report of the global conference on small-scale fisheries: Securing sustainable small-scale fisheries: Bringing together responsible fisheries and social development*. Fisheries and Aquaculture Report No. 911, Rome, 189 pp. Retrieved from www.fao.org/docrep/012/i1227t/i1227t.pdf
FAO. (2016). *The state of world fisheries and aquaculture 2016: Contributing to food security and nutrition for all*. Rome: Author.
Fitriana, R., & Stacey, N. (2012). The role of women in fishery sector of Pantar Island, Indonesia. *Asian Fisheries Science Special Issue, 25S*, 159–175.
Frocklin, S., Torre-Castro, M., Lindstrom, L., & Jiddawi, N. S. (2013). Fish traders as key actors in fisheries: Gender and adaptive management. *Ambio, 42*, 951–962.
Harper, S., Zeller, D., Hauzer, M., Pauly, D., & Sumaila, U. R. (2013). Women and fisheries: Contribution to food security and local economies. *Marine Policy, 39*, 56–63.

Hauzer, M., Dearden, P., & Murray, G. (2013). The fisherwomen of Ngazidja Island, Comoros: Fisheries livelihoods, impacts, and implications for management. *Fisheries Research, 140*, 28–35.

Immanuel, S., & Rao, G. S. (2009). The status of fisherwomen in Andhra Pradesh. *Indian Journal of Gender Studies, 16*(3), 411–423.

Kabeer, N. (1999). Resources, agency, achievements: Reflections on the measurement of women's empowerment. *Development and Change, 30*(3), 435–464.

Kanaga, V., Rajakumar, M., Sivasankar, P., Sruthi, K., & Gowsalya, P. (2015). Constraints analysis in fisherwomen SHGs in Therespuram fishing village, Thoothukudi District. *International Journal of Fisheries and Aquatic Studies, 2*(3), 217–220.

Mallawa, A. (2006). *Pengelolaan Sumberdaya Ikan Berkelanjutan dan Berbasis Masyarakat*. In Lokakarya Agenda Penelitian Program COREMAP II Kabupaten Selayar, 9–10 September 2006.

Pereznieto, P., & Taylor, G. (2014). A review of approaches and methods to measure economic empowerment of women and girls. *Gender & Development, 22*(2), 233–251.

Regulation of the Minister of marine affairs and fisheries of the Republic of Indonesia Number 1 of 2009.

Regulation of the Minister of marine affairs and fisheries of the Republic of Indonesia Number 45 of 2011 on estimation of fishery resources potential in the fishery management area of the Republic of Indonesia.

Weeratunge, N., Snyder, K. A., & Choo, P. S. (2010). Gleaner, fisher, trader, processor: Understanding gendered employment in theories and aquaculture. *Fish and Fisheries, 11*, 406–420.

Williams, M. J. (2008). Why look at fisheries through a gender lens? *Development, 51*, 180–185.

Williams, S. B., Hochet-Kibongui, A. M., & Nauen, C. E. (2005). *Gender, fisheries and aquaculture: Social capital and knowledge for the transition towards sustainable use of aquatic ecosystems*. ACP-EU Fisheries Research Report 16, European Union, Brussels.

Zhao, M., Tyzack, M., Anderson, R., & Onoakpovike, E. (2013). Women as visible and invisible workers in fisheries: A case study of Northern Ireland. *Marine Policy, 37*, 69–76.

The 'Barefoot Model' of economic empowerment in rural Rajasthan

Giulia Mariangela Mininni

ABSTRACT

Social and cultural constraints in remote rural areas alienate women and limit their human development. However, there is potential for engagement in educational and economic activities to support their empowerment and the achievement of wider development goals. I discuss the case study of the Barefoot College from India where illiterate women have been involved for over 20 years in training in small-scale solar energy technology solutions. I argue that the participation in the solar program has the potential to support women's 'effective' and 'transformative' empowerment, as my sample demonstrates. Through the training, poor women have the opportunity to have an income, learn new skills and foster employment opportunities. The engagement with the organization also supports raising their awareness and enables them to become agents of change. By challenging intra-household dynamics and societal customs, women pursue greater empowerment. Due to its unique model, the training program that started in rural Rajasthan scaled up internationally and has been replicated in several countries in south-east Asia, Africa and Latin America.

Introduction

Access to economic resources is an important step towards the empowerment and development of marginalized groups such as women, given gender inequalities in low-income countries. The development literature has recognized the importance of women's individual interests and needs and the importance to avoid homogenization (Chant, 2008; Gallin & Ferguson, 1991; Kabeer, 1999; Maguire, 1984; Momsen, 2001, 2004, 2008; Nussbaum, 2001; Rathgeber, 1990; Safa, 1995; Sharp, Briggs, Yacoub, & Hamed, 2003). However, some common concerns that women in low-income countries face and that can vary according to the cultural and socio-political context are male control of women's work; restricted access of women to economic resources; and undervalued social and political power. They result from a highly unequal distribution of resources between genders, male violence and control over women's sexuality (Kirby, 1999; Schuler, 1986; Sen, 2001).

In order to bridge the economic gap between genders, it can be argued that greater credit should be given to women's roles and responsibilities, along with more power in and outside the household.

The international arena officially recognized the need for a dedicated goal on gender equality and women's empowerment: the new Sustainable Development Goal five, promoting 'gender equality and the empowerment of women and girls' (UNDP, 2016). In light of this goal, debates around the economic empowerment of women to eliminate inequalities and eradicate poverty are fundamental together with more coordinated action between governments and at grass-root level.

Studies show evidence of inequalities such as restricted mobility, high illiteracy, low education, limited skills transfer and low pay in the informal job sector (Klasen & Lamanna, 2009; Ruiz Abril, 2009; Ridgeway, 2011). This is especially true in rural India where women's subordination and oppression due to patriarchal norms and customs are palpable (Calàs, Smircich, & Bourne, 2009; Datta & Gailey, 2012; Ghosh, 2004). Rajasthan is one of the states with the highest percentage of gender discrimination against women in the labor market (Arora, 2012; Singh & Kumud, 2013). In order to address inequalities at global level, these issues should be tackled locally.

It is argued that women's access to resources, also economic, education and employment, has several positive effects for the household as a whole (e.g. better nutrition, improved children's education and health conditions) (Agarwal, 1997; Batliwala, 2015; Kabeer, 2012). The case study of the Solar Mamas program of the Barefoot College, in rural Rajasthan, India, stands testimonial to these claims. By engaging women in educational activities and raising their awareness, they can influence decisions within the household and challenge day-to-day life practices.

I will show how the participation in the solar program contributed to women's effective economic empowerment by providing them with income opportunities. However, the engagement with the Non-governmental Organisation (NGO) also supported transformative empowerment by positively impacting other spheres of their lives.

I will firstly review the literature on women's empowerment, particularly in regards to its economic aspect, in order to explore the implications of income generation on empowerment and gender equality. Secondly, I will discuss key issues identified by the literature such as access to, control over and distribution of resources, and women's bargaining power. I will then explore concerns around employment, social norms and the absence of a legal framework. Finally, I will discuss the findings of the case study.

The concept of empowerment

The term 'empowerment' has different meanings at the conceptual and the methodological levels. Although in feminist and development literature there are several definitions of women's empowerment, most recognize two distinguishing elements: agency and process (Kabeer, 1999; Ibrahim & Alkire, 2007; Malhotra & Schuler, 2005; Sen & Batliwala, 2000). Schuler (1986) identifies empowerment as the process through which women boost their capacity to configure their lives and their surrounding; an evolution in women's conscientization of themselves, of their status and their social interactions. Hence, Schuler highlights the cognitive, psychological and economic processes underlying empowerment, which should operate beyond the legal recognition of rights to safeguard women (Schuler, 1986; Schuler & Kadirgamar-Rajasingham, 1992). On the same note, Humphries (1996, p. 36), refers to:

> ... [I]ncreas[ed] power to ... especially marginalised people and groups, ... those who are farthest down in the ladder in the power over hierarchy and who have least access to knowledge, decisions, networks and resources.

The emphasis is on the individual (or the group) 'self-actualization.' She/he has a leading role in their (her/his) own empowerment (Sen, 1997). Agency expresses people's ability to use resources to their own advantage with the purpose of achieving results that can support them to live the life that they wish. In a broader sense, it also includes the motivation, the meaning and the intention that people have or that is behind actions. Agency also implies seeking networks for collective action. These can be represented by the family, the community, and then, on a wider scale, the market and other institutions.

In relation to empowerment as a process, Kabeer (2003) also distinguishes 'effective' use of agency and 'transformative' use of agency. The first refers to 'women's greater efficiency in carrying out their given roles and responsibilities; the second relates to women's ability to question, challenge and reframe those roles and responsibilities' (Kabeer, 2003, p. 174). When women achieve both, effective and transformative agency, they are able to exercise what is recognized as the strongest form of power in the development arena: the 'power from within' (Rowlands, 1997; Sharp et al., 2003). This kind of power is used when women themselves become active agents by thinking about alternative ways of living (Sharp et al., 2003). These two elements of agency and process are also relevant to women's economic empowerment since, by accessing resources and participating in the job market, women can challenge gender inequalities and initiate a process of transformation.

The definition adopted by Kabeer also refers to the 'ability to make strategic life choices in a context where this ability was previously denied to them' (2001a, p. 19). On this note, Kabeer explains that not all choices have the same relevance in terms of empowerment; 'strategic life choices' support framing other choices in people's day-to-day life (2005). Choices related to the household's income management and control are also key to understand the extent to which women's economic empowerment can support their self-reliance and independence and further empowerment.

Resources and women's bargaining power

Resources (being these material, intellectual, ideological or networks) are enabling factors to empowerment that are acquired through social relations at different levels including the family, the community, the market and the State. Present resources are as important as those that can be expected in future. The latter can be defined as intangible resources that are determined by the rules of resource distribution in the society. Access to these can be allowed or forbidden to certain groups, and hence, establish the boundaries of what can and cannot be chosen.

In relations to the economic aspect of empowerment, I argue that access to income generating resources can certainly play a major role in pursuing other fundamental needs and development goals. However, access to income does not always mean economic empowerment. In order to understand whether women achieve effective or transformative empowerment, it is important to gauge not only the access to but also the control over the resources and what implications and impacts derive for women. For example: how is the money used? Do women have a say? Are women in control of their or the household's income? Who is responsible for it? These concerns are particularly relevant to the Indian context where, even when women have an income, its access and control might be denied by other family members (Kantor, 2003).

Although the women's participation is essential, empowerment is a concept that goes beyond it; it is not a zero-sum game, although there may be winners and losers (Sen, 1998). The bargaining power of a woman within her household might be irrelevant compared to her husband's or in-laws' (Mason & Smith, 2003; Narayan, Chambers, Shah, & Petesch, 2000). There is an extensive literature on bargaining power within and outside the household (Agarwal, 1997; Basu, 2006; Folbre, 1986; Kabeer, 1997; Kandiyoti, 1988; Moser, 1993; Quisumbing & Maluccio, 2003).[1] Gender-based discriminations within other kinds of institutions such as the market and the State are often less overt than in the household and the community (Goetz & World Conference on Women, 1995; Kabeer, 2001b).

Kandiyoti (1988) states: '[w]omen strategize within a set of concrete constraints, which I identify as 'patriarchal bargains' (p. 274). In certain contexts, women take advantage of their subordinate position and adopt strategies that can increase security and improve life options (Kandiyoti, 1988; Sharp et al., 2003). Due to strong cultural norms and customs, and to their vulnerability to those, women are often reluctant to change (Sharp et al., 2003). However, it is still open to discussion the extent to which women are aware that they are adopting such strategies (Kandiyoti, 1988; Sharp et al., 2003).[2] In situations where there are conflicting interests, those with more bargaining power will most probably succeed (Jackson, 1996). Goetz and Gupta (1996) report the example of Bangladeshi women involved in the Grameen Bank and other credit programs for poor rural women. Donors showed more interest in the repayment rate of the loan that women received rather than evaluating their bargaining power within the household. Although women bore the liability for the repayment, men in their household mainly used the loans. In some cases, there was not any evidence of women benefitting from the credit received (Goetz & Gupta, 1996). The same trend has been reported in India (Johnson & Kidder, 1999; Kabeer, 1998; Leach & Sitaram, 2002; Mayoux, 1995). In line with Jackson (1996), the example shows how those with stronger bargaining power within the household can ensure that their interests are satisfied.

In other cases, the achievement of empowerment in one domain undermines or disempowers other areas (Nagar & Raju, 2003). Nagar and Raju (2003), for instance, describe the Mahila Samakhya (women social workers) program in India. Rural women organize in collectives within villages to raise other women's awareness about their rights, political and social issues concerning women. Through the program, women became involved also in education and income generation activities. However, although 'empowering' women in terms of their conscientization and providing them with employment opportunities, some women were paid less than men doing the same job and had to transport daily heavy head-pumps equipment for a long distance (Nagar & Raju, 2003).

Low-paid and hazardous work in the informal sector is very often the only choice for women in India (Desai et al., 2010; Srivastava & Srivastava, 2010). Being responsible for the everyday chores (including childcare, health care and cleaning), and for the satisfaction of basic needs (including water, food and fuel), they are often alienated from specialized science and technology. This ignores and undervalues women's knowledge and experience (Harding, 1986; Haraway, 2013; Sundberg, in press). 'The conflict revolves around the separation of domains of knowledge, as well as the separation of knowing and doing, and the "formal" and "informal" knowledge' (Rocheleau, Thomas-Slayter, & Wangari, 1996, p. 8). Rocheleau (2008), for instance, recognizes multiple dimensions of knowledge and reflects the need to adopt a contextual, holistic and ecological approach to knowledge generation that values this multiplicity. Agarwal (1992), for example, reports on how, although indigenous women have traditional knowledge and experience of plants, soil and agricultural processes, these are 'devaluat[ed] and marginalis[ed]' (p. 135). 'Scientific knowledge' is prioritized with the exclusion of women from it (Agarwal, 1992). In India, examples of rural women's engagement in technology are offered by the Self-Employed Women Association (SEWA). The association engages women in audio-visual training for education and development in Madhya Pradesh (Cecchini & Scott, 2003). In Gujarat, the SEWA started in 2010 IT centers run by rural women with the purpose of networking, therefore fighting isolation, learning and acquiring entrepreneurial skills (IFWSEA, 2015).

While economic development can support women's empowerment, women's access to other kinds of resources (knowledge, information, skills and so on) potentially fosters economic empowerment. Training and managerial roles have often been assigned to men ignoring women's knowledge and practices and excluding them from participating as active agents. Donors and development agencies have frequently only consulted men making women's contribution invisible (Carney, 1992; Schroeder, 1999; Sundberg, in press). Hence, the urgency of addressing gender inequalities in access to science and technology by engaging women in training and income generation programs.

Constraints to women's economic empowerment

As previously discussed, know-how transfer goes hand in hand with better employment conditions for women that contribute to eliminating: discrimination, lower paid jobs and women's segregation. Social security and steady jobs with higher income are some of the factors that potentially benefit women economically (Kabeer, 2012). Chopra and Müller (2016) highlight how the economic element of empowerment 'has been viewed both as a precondition for achieving empowerment as well as the indicator for the achievement of this goal' (Chopra & Müller, 2016, p. 3).

Women's participation in the employment realm is also influenced by social norms and customs. These operate in the market, the State and other institutions though they are shaped by gender roles of production and reproduction and power relations within the household (Goetz & World Conference on Women, 1995 ; Kabeer, 1994). The domination of women is evident in the private and public spheres. Forms of subordination may include violence exercised by the husband, women's acceptance of secondary claims to resources, preference for sons and so on (Kabeer, 2001b). Other forms of domination might include acceptance of lower wages and informal work, and lower attendance to school. Vinkenburg (2015) suggests that women's economic empowerment can be achieved only by changing and re-thinking these norms, values and their impact. Some authors identify the need for systems in place, including childcare, job stability and so on, to support the market economy (Chopra, 2015).

Since women in most low-income countries occupy multiple roles, productive, repro-ductive and caring (Moser, 1989, 1993; Moser & Levy, 1986), their contribution to the household's income is taken for granted by the society, their family and the community. Also, personal bias, interpretation of the reality, its norms and customs, might play a key role in influencing people's agency towards changing those. The gender and well-being literature suggests that many women have internalized their status as persons of lesser value inside and outside the household (Kabeer, 2001a). This has significant consequences for them and other female family members (Kabeer, 2001a). Therefore, although achieving effective empowerment in their triple-role, some women lack awareness or the capacity to challenge social norms and pursue transformative empowerment. People's empowerment starts when they understand, critically analyze and then challenge 'social borders' that constrain their lives and dictate the conditions under which they live (Hayward, 2000). This critical analysis is aimed at elaborating a strategy to change these conditions. Mose-dale (2003, p. 2) states: 'empowerment cannot be bestowed by a third party.'

Another constraint to women's economic empowerment is the lack of a legal frame-work supporting women's rights. Gender and equality theories seek a more just system dealing with the distribution of rights, power and money between men and women since legal and political asymmetrical structures might obstruct women's empowerment and sustainable development goals (Skutsch, 2005; Unterhalter, 2005; cited in Mininni, 2014).

Uneven distribution of rights and responsibilities is gendered in relation to space, private and public spheres. Due to patriarchal property rights men dominate the control, access and allocation of resources such as land (Rocheleau et al., 1996). Also, as discussed before, labor obligations within the family prevent women from participating in and benefitting from sustainable development programs. The recognition of gendered rights and spaces highlights the need to reform the traditional divisions of labor and the separation between public and private realms. Some feminists also call for a platform for women to pursue their empowerment through collective action (Batliwala, 2015). This can enable societal and structural transformation that can bring about long lasting change (Batliwala, 2015). Women's collective action to build networks is the main tool to challenge subordination and it is on the basis of the majority of women's empowerment strategies (Kabeer, UN, & UNRISD, 1999; Mosedale, 2003; Stromquist, 1999). Hence, again, the above discussion highlights the importance of women's transformative agency to achieve greater empowerment.

I argue that rural women's participation in training programs on skills and knowledge transfer can support women's effective economic empowerment by offering income gen-eration opportunities. Moreover, NGOs can play a key role in promoting women's transfor-mative agency. This can happen by raising their awareness and creating an enabling environment for women to start their empowerment process that can also impact other spheres of their lives.

The solar mamas program of the barefoot college

The Barefoot College is a NGO based in Rajasthan, which believes that the empowerment of socially marginalized and deprived individuals, such as rural women, is essential for the development of remote communities (Barefoot College, 2015a). The organization follows

Gandhi's life and work style and supports his principles such as that knowledge and skills should be found within the community rather than coming from external sources (Barefoot College, 2015a).

One of their programs, the Solar Mamas, focuses on small-scale energy photo voltaic (PV) home systems, solar cookers and solar lanterns. The program can be considered as an example of good practice of community-based approach for community engagement. The organization engages illiterate women in training on the building, operation and maintenance of PV systems with the aims of: contributing to their empowerment and income generation (through skills transfer, illiterate women participate in the design, implementation and operation of energy projects); transferring technology to rural areas and ensuring that this is operated and maintained by local communities; 'strong [ly] commit[ting] to developing women as agents of sustainable change'; and supporting 'communities to develop their own capacity to meet the challenges within the developing world' (Barefoot College, 2015a, p. 1, 2015b; Beri, 2011; Elkington & Hartigan, 2013; Mohideen, 2012; Oparaocha & Dutta, 2011; Practical Action, 2013; Rojas, Schmitt, & Aguilar, 2012; Roy, 2011; Santos, 2012).

According to the 2006 Rajasthan Development Report, underemployment is prevalent in rural areas where people rely on rainfall for agricultural activities. This creates high levels of uncertainty in relation to livelihood security since animal husbandry and agriculture are the main resources in Rajasthan (PCGI, 2002). Gender discrimination in Rajasthan is also evident in relation to female literacy with the lowest rate in India (Singh & Kumud, 2013). Given that by law and customs Rajasthan follows a patrilinear system, also in terms of inheritance and land ownership, there is a consistent discrimination against female children (PGCI, 2002). Such trend led to the diffusion of female feticide and infanticide practices although these are considered illegal by the Indian central government (Tandon & Sharma, 2006). Unequal distribution of resources happens also in relation to food and nutrition, education, rights and health care (Tandon & Sharma, 2006).

The College offers training and employment to otherwise unemployed and marginalized rural women and offers them alternative scenarios to their segregation.

The 'Barefoot Model' of '[e]ducating local people through peer-to-peer learning is transformational in that it relies on the passing on of traditional skills and knowledge' rather than relying on outsiders to bring in new methods (Barefoot College, 2012).

The founder Bunker Roy states: '[t]he model has taken into account the pace at which people think, the culture, which is respected, and the capacity … of the community to adjust to, apply and to disseminate ideas' (Barefoot College, 2012). 'That's what scalability is all about. It's a model that people understand; it's not complicated. It respects the skills that people have rather than discarding them or replacing them' (Barefoot College, 2012). The model developed over the years ensures a bottom-up approach based on indigenous knowledge and community engagement. The College is now operating its model of solar electrification, clean water, education and livelihood development to rural communities in over 70 countries in the global south.

I will explore the Solar Mamas program in detail in the analysis section. I will evaluate whether, due to the engagement in the Solar Mamas program, women were able to exercise effective and transformative agency, and how this contributed to their empowerment.

Methods and case study design

I explored the implementation of the Solar Mamas' program in the Ajmer District in Rajasthan because in this rural area women's subordination is palpable due to traditions, customs and social norms (O'Reilly, 2006; Duflo, 2012; Pankaj & Tankha, 2010; Singh & Kumud, 2013).

I adopted a mixed methods feminist approach to data collection by: 'reducing the hierarchical relationship between researchers and their participants to facilitate trust and disclosure[;] recognizing and reflecting upon the emotionality of women's lives'; consulting documents, reports and videos available through the NGO archive (Campbell & Wasco, 2000, abstract). During the fieldwork, I also carried out semi-structured interviews and focus groups.[3] For the purpose of this article, I analyzed 33 interviews. I selected participants using non-probability sampling, either because of the position they hold (e.g. professionals from the NGO) or because of the particular or unique contribution they made (e.g. I interviewed the first solar engineer that has been working at the organization for over 20 years) (Burnham, Lutz, Grant, & Layton-Henry, 2008; Creswell, 2012). A limitation of small samples is the difficulty to make inferences about the wider population with small sample sizes (Crouch & McKenzie, 2006). However, in-depth interviews with a limited number of people can allow a more reflective and personal account (Crouch & McKenzie, 2006).

In order to analyze the data collected, I referred to the data analysis literature (Caudle, 2004; Dey, 2003; Gibbs, 2002; Yin, 2011, 2015) that suggests using patterns of concepts and categories using classification and interconnection to explore the main issues and develop conclusions. This is a technique used in qualitative data analysis that eases the categorization process of data for interpretation.

I started by identifying key themes on the basis of the gender and women's empowerment literature that I believed are relevant to my study (Hashemi, Schuler, & Riley, 1996; Jejeebhoy, 2003; Kabeer, 1999; Kishor, 1997; Longwe, 1995; March, Smyth, & Mukhopadhyay, 1999). These include: the women's and energy nexus; women's effective and transformative agency; and changes and challenges in women's lives. In order to select the main themes, I especially referred to studies related to the measurement of women's empowerment and adapted the key concepts to my study (Charmes & Wieringa, 2003; Kabeer, 1999; Kabeer et al., 1999; Kandpal, Baylis, & Arends-Kuenning, 2013; Mosedale, 2003; Williams, 2005; Narayan et al., 2000). Then, while exploring women's accounts, I identified three sets of women interviewees: the solar trainees that became solar teachers within the Barefoot College, the solar trainees that became solar engineers and went back to their villages and the solar cookers engineers. These three sets of interviewees have been differently impacted by the participation in the solar training program also in terms of their economic empowerment.

I interviewed 9 solar teachers, 12 solar engineers and 6 solar cookers engineers. Since not all them replied to all the questions, I reported the analysis of the findings by thematic area. Firstly, I assessed women's expectations and the benefits that derived by the training: their involvement in the training, whether income and employment opportunities were among their expectations and among the benefits deriving from it. Why did women get involved? Did they choose independently? Were they seizing financial opportunities? Secondly, I evaluated women's control over resources and their participation in decision-making. The discussion refers to the changes that happened after the training, women's responsibility for the income, including their salary, its use and their level of independence. Through their engagement in the training and their work afterwards, women gained a salary. However, my analysis evaluates also the extent to which their economic empowerment had further transformational impacts in their lives. Were women then able to influence decisions at home? Were they in charge of their salary and what was it used for? Thirdly, I gauged women's understanding of empowerment: whether the economic aspect was important to them and their level of awareness of the empowerment process. Finally, I considered whether they achieved transformative empowerment and what other areas of their lives are influenced by it.

Issues with measuring empowerment

The open-ended nature of empowerment as a process poses challenges in regard to its measurement. Difficulties arise since it possible to be empowered in relation to one aspect of people's life (for instance in terms of economic self-reliance) and yet still facing inequality in respect to other aspects (for example in relation to the freedom of choice). Hence, by examining empowerment goals, it is possible to measure its outcomes or achievements. When measuring women's empowerment, it is important to consider that this is not a binary process: empowerment versus disempowerment. Therefore, it is difficult to measure women's empowerment according to the level of conformity to indicators (Kabeer, 2001a). Considering instead the 'expansion in people's choices,' it is possible to gauge the level of women's engagement in decision-making, and hence, the priorities identified by them in the empowerment process (Kabeer, 2001a).

I refer to Kishor's (1997 as cited in Kabeer, 1999, p. 449) analysis of empowerment in regards to its measurement since she interprets empowerment as: women's 'control' over resources (also economic including earnings and household's finances), women's 'self-reliance' (the ability of women to be economically independent) and 'decision-making' (also in regards to income).

Analysis of women's economic empowerment

Before discussing the findings, I will explore distinctive aspects of the three Solar Mamas' programs (the solar teachers, the solar engineers and the solar cookers engineers), since those have differently impacted women. When participating in the program, women are trained for six months. Usually, the solar teachers either live on campus or in nearby villages; the same is for the solar cookers engineers. The solar engineers, instead, go back to their villages to install the solar panels. The solar teachers' and the solar cookers engineers' salary is paid by the College. The salary of the solar engineers is paid by the partner organization that supports them and by the local communities. Once the solar engineers install the panels, the communities repay them in a lump sum or in installments over a period of three years. Unless requiring maintenance (if the panel is somehow damaged), or technologic upgrade, usually the batteries are changed every 5–7 years. The life span of the panels is of more than 25 years; therefore they require little maintenance.

The solar teachers

Working as solar teachers offers several advantages: the continuity of salary allows women to become more independent from their husbands or in-laws over time; hence, achieving a more transformative empowerment; the engagement in the NGO provides a safe environment; the kind of work is not heavy and it is safe; women are integrated into the job market; and there are no social inequalities depending on gender, class, social status, religion or caste.

The solar engineers

Since the engineers' salary is supposedly paid by the local partner organization, with a contribution from the community for the maintenance of the panels as explained before, I explored to what extent women received support and whether the engineers encountered any issues during or after the training. Lack of work, discontinuity and low pay were among the comments of eight of the interviewees, who suggested improvement of the program in these regards. Some women received more support than others by the partner organizations and have been integrated into working on other projects. Once the community repays the panels, the partner organizations have to rely on other funds to support the engineers. Therefore, there is no continuity in their salaries after the first one to two years. Moreover, the interviews with professionals from the organizations revealed that, although usually communities repay promptly since solar electrification is in their own interest, there have been some issues with repayment. While during the training at the college women are assured the minimum wage, after the training, some of the women are paid less; therefore, they opt for government jobs. This supposedly depends on the organization's availability of external funds, which translates in smaller salaries or in part-time work for women.

The findings show women's willingness to work since they felt that earning would have contributed to their independence, self-esteem and to the well-being of their family. Indeed, involvement in the training and employment opportunity for women, even if for a short term, can still have other positive consequences in women's lives. A study from Jensen (2010), for instance, reports on an employment program involving women in rural north India; three years after the start of the program, 5% more girls and female adolescents enrolled in schools (Jensen, 2010 cited in Duflo, 2012).

The solar cookers engineers

The solar cookers engineers acquired specific skills in order to build the cookers; moreover, they set up the first Women Barefoot Solar Cookers Engineers Society (WBSCES). During the training, the engineers learnt many technical skills such as operation and functioning of the mechanical pendulum clocks, different kinds of solar cookers and how to use more than 50 different tools (Kakani, 2014). Furthermore, they learnt about complex concepts such as latitude and location and how to weld and assemble 300 mirrors (Kakani, 2014). By managing the society, women also learnt many entrepreneurial skills such as accountancy, management, purchasing, sales and budgeting (Kakani, 2014). The solar cookers engineers became multi-skilled and the engagement in the WBSCES for them also meant infringing social customs and being exposed to new challenges. This point will be discussed more deeply in the session on the infringement of social norms.

Theme 1: Expectations and benefits

In the interviews, most of the solar teachers identified income, employment and autonomy among their expectations. One solar teacher stated:

> I am from a very poor background and I needed some money. I am happy that now also women from lower class without education can be employed.

Also, another stated: '[w]hat the Barefoot College does is great since women receive a salary to study. Other institutions ask for fees.' The solar engineering training offers the unique opportunity to rural women to be paid while training and to receive a salary while working as solar teachers or engineers. The majority of the teachers referred to increased income as a benefit, together with autonomy and employment. In terms of the changes that happened in women's lives after the training, one of the teachers mentioned how the training contributed to her own sustainability and independence.

Most of the solar engineers expected increased income, employment opportunities, control and autonomy. One solar engineer had to join the training since she was a widow and another one was separated; since they did not have any other income, they thought that the solar program could be a good opportunity for them to improve their finances. One Solar Mama said: 'I learnt new skills, got an income, met new people and did not have to do a heavy job.' The safety aspect of the job seems to be relevant since rural women often find themselves working in hazardous conditions due to the lack of security measures in the workplace and gender sensitive policies.

Most engineers as well recognized income, employment and autonomy as benefits together with increased control. In particular, one solar engineer said that she was proud of being an entrepreneur now.

The solar cookers engineers expected income, employment and increased autonomy.

I then asked what benefits derived from the participation. As above, also the solar cookers engineers referred to autonomy, employment and income as benefits received. One explicitly referred to income as an important reason for her well-being: '[w]ith money everything is alright,' she said. While having a direct impact on women's lives, by providing them with a salary, women also found other benefits deriving by the program that positively impacted their lives beyond just economic gains.

Theme 2: Control over income and decision-making

One teacher said that she was in control of the income and that this has always been the case. Three other teachers said that their family was in charge of the income, although two of them had a say. Two solar engineers declared that the decision-making has not changed since they were already participating in it. Other three solar engineers said that their husbands or their in-laws took decisions with two women declaring that they did not even have a say. One of those said that she would have liked to be consulted. For the majority of the solar cookers engineers, the control over the income is shared with their husbands. Two of them said that they are in charge of it. Also, the decision-making within the household is mostly shared.

It seems like not many changes happened in women's lives in relation to their decision-making within the household. Perhaps, this happened since these kinds of changes require long-term negotiations and challenging preconceptions within the family.

In terms of responsibility for women's salaries, most teachers said that the responsibility for the salary is shared with family members. For the engineers, the findings are split between a few women who were in charge of their own salary and the same amount of women with their family taking charge. One solar engineer said that the in-laws were in charge of her salary and they gave her a token. This is not surprising though given that usually in India people live in extended families with male heads of the household, either the father, or brothers-in-law, or the husband (Kantor, 2003). Two women did not finish the training; therefore, they did not have a salary. Most of the solar cookers engineers shared the management of their salaries with their families. Two women said that they were responsible for it.

Another area of investigation has been how the salary is used. Other studies (Kabeer, 1999; Kabeer et al., 1999) report that usually women spend most of their income for the family and their children rather than for personal items. This has been the case of the solar teachers; five of them replied that their income was used for their children, especially to ensure their education. Two teachers said that their husbands contributed equally with their incomes and only one said that her income was used for the enlarged family. In regards to the solar engineers, five of them used their salaries for their children and for the households' management, including buying food. However, one woman used her income towards buying some land and a house; another said that she used her salary to build a shelter for the goats; and another bought a radio and a mobile. Surprisingly, half of the engineers used part of the salary also to purchase personal items such as jewels and dresses. Only one engineer said that she used it to repay her husband's debts since she was forced to do so. He was unemployed, used to drink and was violent towards her. Four solar cookers engineers used their salaries for their children's education and five for the house management, including food. Only one said that the salary benefitted the enlarged family.

In relation to women's responsibility for their own salary and how it is used, there is evidence of both, effective and transformative empowerment. Some women used the salary for domestic purposes; whether or not this was their choice, it is difficult to gauge. Other women showed a greater level of independence and autonomy in deciding upon what items to purchase and for whom.

Theme 3: Understanding of empowerment

I then asked what the interviewees' understanding of empowerment was and whether other areas of their lives have been impacted by it. For the purposes of this paper, I will discuss only the aspects related to the economic empowerment. I firstly analyzed the data related to the solar teachers. One of the teachers stated:

> Women do not have to ask for money to their husband ... As both husband and wife are earning, it adds lots of value since things are getting more and more expensive.

Another teacher explained how beneficial working was for her since she had a say, became independent, had an income and had knowledge. She would have never imagined that she could do these things. The results of the investigation show how six of the teachers included economic gain and employability as components of their empowerment and they related it to other concepts such as 'independence' and 'knowledge.'

Secondly, I asked about the solar engineers' understanding of women's economic empowerment. The engineers referred to financial stability, independence and improvement in the quality of their lives. In response to the question on what empowerment meant to them, one engineer stated:

> The expenditures will be shared, the financial conditions will improve and overall it will affect the standard of living in the house. Definitely, both husband and wife will live as partners. I would be independent and wouldn't have to beg for money to my husband.

Another engineer stated: 'I have been working and made a difference. I feel respected and recognized by my community.' Increased independence and ability to make their own choices as indexes of empowerment are evident also from the example offered by one of the interviewees: ' … to be financially independent, make my own choices and buy the clothes that I want.' One woman told how the involvement in the training program was an opportunity for women's empowerment; she could see that this was happening for other women as well in the program.

Finally, I evaluated the findings regarding the solar cookers engineers. Most of the women related to their increased independence improved confidence and ability to satisfy their wishes. One interviewee referred to her increased purchasing power by saying: 'I can buy beauty products, jewels and bangles for myself now without asking for permission.' Similarly, another engineer said:

> This is a totally new experience for me. For fifteen years I have only been at home looking after my children. Muslim women are not allowed outside their houses. Since I started working I felt good. I don't need to ask my husband for money.

These quotes highlight the increased level of women's independence and how participating in the program was a revelation to these women. The quotes though also refer to the 'patriarchal bargains' that women have to cope within societies dominated by men. Asking for permission to move outside the house and to purchase items is a common rule in rural Rajasthan. Due to the participation in the program, some women are now aware of the possibilities available to them. They referred to concepts such as equality and autonomy. Hence, they have started that conscientization and transformative process to achieve greater empowerment in their lives.

Theme 4: Impact of economic empowerment in the participants' lives

Infringement of social norms

In order to attend the training, some women had to challenge social norms. Five teachers faced opposition to join the program either from their family or their community. Some of them had to challenge the purdah and cannot speak in front of the elders. One teacher said that she stopped wearing the ghagra[4] and opted instead for a saree. The latter is more neutral and does not reveal which community she belonged to. She was happier at the College. According to traditions, women are not allowed to work outside their household or even speak in front of the elders of the family.

Although for half of the engineers interviewed it was their choice to join the program, six women faced opposition by their families or communities before starting the training. They had to challenge preconceptions and biases dictated by societal customs. One of the women talked about how her in-laws opposed to her wish to join the training and about the compromises she had to face. She had to leave her children at her mother's place. However, she was determined to learn and get an income.

Another engineer said:

> I challenged social norms since I am separated, I work with men, I don't cover my head with the palluh and I am taking lifts on the bikes. People pointed the finger at me.

One solar engineer explains how the community opinions were actually split due to her social status, and she had to find ways to convince them. These kinds of negotiations within the household and within the community, as reported in the literature on women's empowerment (Agarwal, 1997; Cornwall, 2003; Kabeer et al., 1999), require great self-determination.

At the start of the program, the solar cookers engineers faced rejection by local steel traders. Due to traditional customs in Rajasthan, women are not allowed to approach traders by themselves. Socially constructed gender preconceptions about the division of labor influence women's engagement in economic activities. Some of the women mentioned that working at the college was really challenging in terms of breaking social norms. An engineer stated: '[so] women are not limited to the kitchen only.' To assemble the solar parabolic cooker, the solar cookers engineers learnt how to weld, and welding is usually done by a specific low caste in India; therefore, some family members and communities could not accept their engagement with the project.

Social integration

Participating in the program also contributed to integrating those women that were otherwise isolated and marginalized. One teacher cites: 'I was feeling very lonely at home, so I thought that by working I could have felt better.' Another teacher also stated:

> I am free to move around and I have a say now. I earned it by working at the Barefoot College, so my family cannot say anything to me.

The engineers' awareness about the spectrum of activities that women can engage with has increased. One solar engineer reported that there is some availability of work; however, women do not become involved since in the villages they are not allowed outside the house. This is due to women's segregation and isolation in rural areas. However, participating in the solar program for her meant: 'I got an opportunity to grow and to do what it is traditionally believed that men only can do.' Another engineer also said: 'I feel that this is usually a job that men would do; but actually, when you start to learn it is not that difficult.' These are statements to the challenges that women face and to the awareness that they develop by being engaged in the Solar Mamas' program.

One solar cooker engineer had some health issues that were aggravating by staying at home isolated. Engaging with the program she met new people, learnt new skills and contributed to the household's income.

Further working and training opportunities

I then explored the extent to which the solar program triggered women's agency in terms of their interest in pursuing other income generation activities and receiving further training. To what extent has the program been transformative in these regards?

Three teachers already engaged with a partner NGO or doing some independent electrical engineering work. Most of them were satisfied with their income and activity. After the training, one of the teachers became the coordinator of a rural center and has been working there since 1997.

Seven solar engineers were yet engaged in other activities as midwives with the partner organizations, on family farms or in animal husbandry. Since there has been no continuity and stability of income, the solar engineers felt more vulnerable in terms of their economic self-reliance. Hence, they need to pursue other income generation activities.

The solar cookers engineers did not show interested in other jobs since they have a stable income and they are satisfied with their work. The solar teachers, as well as the solar cookers engineers, enjoy several advantages by being involved in the program: they have a stable income, social security, are engaged with the community at the College and do a job most of the women never thought they could do. Part of those benefits is also experienced by some of the solar engineers involved with partner organizations.

In terms of learning new skills to enhance their employability, the solar teachers showed interest in engaging in more training on electrical engineering or on solar energy.

Seven engineers would like to receive further training in computer or on other skills that could provide them with an income, such as tailoring, embroidery and so on. Only two of the solar cookers engineers are willing to engage in further training: one to improve the solar cookers and another in whatever the NGO suggests to her.

The analysis of the findings provides evidence about transformative agency for some women since they challenged other areas and practices in their daily lives either than securing an income. However, the findings also show some of the limitations to the Solar Mamas program. Lack of job continuity is evident for some women. Since the responsibility of providing the salaries after the training shifts on the partner organizations, it can be questioned why the NGO trains other women as solar engineers once the sustainability of their employment cannot be guaranteed. Constraints to employing the same group of women over different locations might be represented by transport, mobility issues and eventual mistrust or hostility by new communities who are unknown to the Solar Mamas. However, training more women means providing income and employability skills to more people, raising awareness of more women, and engaging otherwise marginalized and oppressed groups. In the long term, these benefits could impact also other spheres of their lives as showed when discussing the findings. What would be ideal in terms of promoting better self-reliance for the solar engineers is more support from the partner organizations to provide women with those skills that can enable them to start off other livelihoods activities. Examples of skills would be networking, community assets mapping, and leadership. These limitations have been recognized by the organization that is developing solutions. The College lately started, together with its partners, complementing the solar program with workshops on livelihood and entrepreneurial skills for women in order to implement activities locally (Barefoot College, 2015a). The engagement of women in this integrated program can enable the process to achieve that transformation that leads to their greater empowerment and to the empowerment of other women. However further research and interviews will be needed in the future in order to ascertain whether this solution is effective.

Conclusions

The analysis of the findings shows the interconnection between women's empowerment and economic development. However, it also demonstrates that access and control over resources alone cannot be parameters of empowerment. This is true especially in a context such as rural India, where strong social conventions that nourish discrimination against women are embedded in the culture. It is important to enquire the process behind the access and control over economic gains, the negotiations and the compromises that women make in their households with their family members and that enable them to access and control resources.

Even when women declare that they led their own empowerment process and that the choices made were personal, it is challenging to gauge and understand whether these were conscious choices, or whether they were unconsciously biased by the socio-cultural norms and context (e.g. decision-making over the use of the income could be influenced by the family as it is custom in Rajasthan for women to abide their families' will). Attending the training for some women meant challenging cultural norms of rural Rajasthan where 'constraints' in women's lives due to traditions are palpable.

Hence, this study shows how women's economic empowerment not only influences the economic sphere, but also others by contributing to, for instance, challenging social customs, increasing independence and acquiring employability skills. When these elements are in place, women can feel empowered to take initiatives that they would have not otherwise considered before, such as for example, engaging in new income gen-erating activities with other organizations or at home.

The Barefoot College offered the opportunity to women participating in the solar program to engage with technologic innovations and learn new skills. As discussed when reviewing the literature, women's alienation from science and technology is usually a gap in the development arena. The NGO is participatory, non-hierarchical, adopts rural strategies to development by favoring a learning-by-doing approach. The organization is also innovative by challenging practices there were limitations are found. Therefore, it would be interesting to explore the scope of the new livelihood program launched by the organization, the impact on the women involved and the com-munities affected by it, and the extent to which it could challenge social norms and promote transformative empowerment.

The Solar Mamas are exemplary to other women from the majority world since some of the issues that they face in terms of inequality and disempowerment, as discussed, are the same. They inspire other women that attend the training every year, and they are the evidence of what women, although illiterate, and although living in rural areas are capable of doing with the support from institutions. These are some of the reasons why the 'Barefoot Model' has been replicated in over 70 countries in the global south.

Notes

1. The literature on masculinity also emphasises how some men dislike the idea of women within their family to be empowered (Cornwall, 1997).
2. Kandiyoti (1988) also specifies that the exercise of 'patriarchal bargains' might vary according to status, class, ethnicity and caste (this is particularly true in India for instance); they impact women's passive or active roles as agents of change in relations to their oppression and they are historically and geographically subject to transformation and renegotiation.
3. Keele University, the Keele University Postgraduate Association (KPA) bursary, the Santander Bank travel fund, the Athena Swan fund and the UK India Education Research Initiative (UKIERI) fellowship sponsored the fieldwork for this study.
4. The ghagra choli is a traditional dress that women wear in rural areas in northern Indian states. Women belonging to the same community wear similar dresses with patterns, colours and accessories.

Disclosure statement

No potential conflict of interest was reported by the author.

References

Agarwal, B. (1992). The gender and environment debate: Lessons from India. *Feminist Studies*, *18*(1), 119–158.

Agarwal, B. (1997). 'Bargaining' and gender relations: Within and beyond the household. *Feminist Economics*, *3*(1), 1–51.

Arora, R. U. (2012). Gender inequality, economic development, and globalization: A state level analysis of India. *The Journal of Developing Areas*, *46*(1), 147–164.

Barefoot College. (2012). *Disrupting poverty: How Barefoot college is empowering women … .* Retrieved from https://www.barefootcollege.org/disrupting-poverty-how-barefoot-college-is-empowering-women.

Barefoot College. (2015a). *Annual report*. Retrieved from https://www.barefootcollege.org.

Barefoot College. (2015b). *Volunteer form*. Retrieved from https://www.barefootcollege.org.

Basu, K. (2006). Gender and say: A model of household behaviour with endogenously determined balance of *power*. *The Economic Journal*, *116*(511), 558–580.

Batliwala, S. (2015). *Engaging with empowerment: An intellectual and experiential journey*. New Delhi: Women Unlimited.

Beri, R. (2011). *Evolving India-Africa relations: continuity and change*. South African Institute of International Affairs. Berilin: Konrad-Adenauer-Stiftung.

Burnham, P., Lutz, K. G., Grant, W., & Layton-Henry, Z. (2008). *Research methods in politics*. Basingstoke, Hampshire: Palgrave Macmillan.

Calàs, M. B., Smircich, L., & Bourne, K. A. (2009). Extending the boundaries: Reframing 'entrepreneurship as social change' through feminist perspectives. *Academy of Management Review, 34*(3), 552–569.

Campbell, R., & Wasco, S. M. (2000). Feminist approaches to social science: Epistemological and methodological tenets. *American Journal of Community Psychology, 28*(6), 773–791.

Carney, J. A. (1992). Peasant women and economic transformation in the Gambia. *Development and Change, 23*(2), 67–90.

Caudle, S. L. (2004). Qualitative data analysis. *Handbook of Practical Program Evaluation, 2*, 417–438.

Cecchini, S., & Scott, C. (2003). Can information and communications technology applications contribute to poverty reduction? Lessons from rural India. *Information Technology for Development, 10*(2), 73–84.

Chant, S. (2008). The 'feminisation of poverty' and the 'feminisation' of anti-poverty programmes: Room for revision? *The Journal of Development Studies, 44*(2), 165–197.

Charmes, J., & Wieringa, S. (2003). Measuring women's empowerment: An assessment of the gender-related development index and the gender empowerment measure. *Journal of Human Development, 4*(3), 419–435.

Chopra, D. (2015). Balancing paid work and unpaid care work to achieve women's economic empowerment. *IDS, Policy Briefing, 83*(January), 1–4.

Chopra, D., & Müller, C., Eds. (2016). Connecting perspectives on women's empowerment. *IDS Bulletin, Transforming Development Knowledge, 47*(1A), 1–10.

Cornwall, A. (1997). Men, masculinity and 'gender in development'. *Gender & Development, 5*(2), 8–13.

Cornwall, A. (2003). Whose voices? Whose choices? Reflections on gender and participatory development. *World Development, 31*(8), 1325–1342.

Creswell, J. W. (2012). *Qualitative inquiry and research design. Choosing among five approaches* (3rd ed). Los Angeles, CA: Sage.

Crouch, M., & McKenzie, H. (2006). The logic of small samples in interview-based qualitative research. *Social Science Information, 45*(4), 483–499.

Datta, P. B., & Gailey, R. (2012). Empowering women through social entrepreneurship: Case study of a women's cooperative in India. *Entrepreneurship Theory and Practice, 36*(3), 569–587.

Desai, S. B., Dubey, A., Joshi, B. L., Sen, M., Shariff, A., & Vanneman, R. (2010). *Human development in India* (pp. 12–12). New Delhi: Oxford University Press.

Dey, I. (2003). *Qualitative data analysis: A user-friendly guide for social scientists*. London: Routledge.

Duflo, E. (2012). Women empowerment and economic development. *Journal of Economic Literature, 50*(4), 1051–1079.

Elkington, J., & Hartigan, P. (2013). *The power of unreasonable people: How social entrepreneurs create markets that change the world*. Boston, MA: Harvard Business Press.

Folbre, N. (1986). Hearts and spades: Paradigms of household economics. *World Development, 14*(2), 245–255.

Gallin, R. S., & Ferguson, A. (1991). *The women and international development annual: Volume 2*. Boulder, CO: Westview Press.

Ghosh, J. (2004). Globalization, export-oriented employment for women and social policy: A case study of India. In *Globalization, export-oriented employment and social policy* (pp. 91–125). London: Palgrave Macmillan.

Gibbs, G. (2002). *Qualitative data analysis: Explorations with NVivo (understanding social research)*. Buckingham: Open University Press.

Goetz, A. M., & Gupta, R. S. (1996). Who takes the credit? Gender, power, and control over loan use in rural credit programs in Bangladesh. *World Development, 24*(1), 45–63.

Goetz, A. M., & World Conference on Women. (1995). *The politics of integrating gender to state development processes: Trends, opportunities and constraints in Bangladesh, Chile, Jamaica, Mali, Morocco and Uganda*. Geneva: United Nations Research Institute for Social Development.

Haraway, D. (2013). *Simians, cyborgs, and women: The reinvention of nature*. New York, NY: Routledge.

Harding, S. G. (1986). *The science question in feminism*. Ithaca, NY: Cornell University Press.

Hashemi, S. M., Schuler, S. R., & Riley, A. P. (1996). Rural credit programs and women's empowerment in Bangladesh. *World Development, 24*(4), 635–653.

Hayward, C. R. (2000). *De-facing power*. Cambridge: Cambridge University Press.

Humphries, B. (1996). *Critical perspectives on empowerment*. Birmingham: Venture.

Ibrahim, S., & Alkire, S. (2007). Agency and empowerment: A proposal for internationally comparable indicators. *Oxford Development Studies, 35*(4), 379–403.

International Federation of Workers' Education Association (IFWSEA). (2015). *Homepage*. Retrieved from http://www.ifwea.org/?x637150=826726.

Jackson, C. (1996). Rescuing gender from the poverty trap. *World Development, 24*(3), 489–504.

Jejeebhoy, S. J. (2000). Women's autonomy in rural India: Its dimensions, determinants, and the influence of context. In H. Presser & G. Sen (Eds.), *Women's empowerment and demographic process. Moving beyond Cairo* (pp. 204–238). Oxford: Oxford University Press.

Jensen, R. T. (2010). *Economic opportunities and gender differences in human capital: Experimental evidence for India*. Working Paper (No. w16021). Cambridge, MA: National Bureau of Economic Research.

Johnson, S., & Kidder, T. (1999). Globalization and gender-dilemmas for microfinance organizations. *Small Enterprise Development, 10*(3), 4–15.

Kabeer, N. (1994). *Reversed realities: Gender hierarchies in development thought*. London: Verso.

Kabeer, N. (1997). Women, wages and intra-household power relations in urban Bangladesh. *Development and Change, 28*(2), 261–302.

Kabeer, N. (1998). *'Money can't buy me love'? Re-evaluating gender, credit and empowerment in rural Bangladesh*. Discussion Paper. Brighton: Institute of Development Studies, University of Sussex.

Kabeer, N. (1999). Resources, agency, achievements: Reflections on the measurement of women's empowerment. *Development and Change, 30*(3), 435–464.

Kabeer, N. (2001a). Conflicts over credit: Re-evaluating the empowerment potential of loans to women in rural Bangladesh. *World Development, 29*(1), 63–84.

Kabeer, N. (2001b). Reflections on the measurement of women's empowerment. In A. Sisask (Ed.), *Discussing women's empowerment: Theory and practice* (pp. 17–54). Stockholm: SIDA.

Kabeer, N. (2003). Gender equality and women's empowerment. In N. Kabeer (Ed.), *Gender mainstreaming in poverty eradication and the MDGs: A handbook for policymakers and other stakeholders* (pp. 169–195). Ottawa: Commonwealth Secretariat/IDRC/CIDA.

Kabeer, N. (2005). Gender equality and women's empowerment: A critical analysis of the third millennium development goal 1. *Gender & Development, 13*(1), 13–24.

Kabeer, N. (2012). *Women's economic empowerment and inclusive growth: Labour markets and enterprise development*. Discussion Paper 29/12. London: International Development Research Centre.

Kabeer, N., United Nations (UN), & United Nations Research Institute for Social Development (UNRISD). (1999). *The conditions and consequences of choice: Reflections on the measurement of women's empowerment* (Vol. 108, pp. 1–58). Geneva: UNRISD.

Kakani, M. (2014). *The women barefoot solar cooker engineers (WBSCE) booklet*. Tilonia: Barefoot College.

Kandiyoti, D. (1988). Bargaining with patriarchy. *Gender & Society, 2*(3), 274–290.

Kandpal, E., Baylis, K., & Arends-Kuenning, M. (2013). *Measuring the effect of a community-level program on women's empowerment outcomes: Evidence from India*. Policy Research Working Paper (6399). Washington: World Bank.

Kantor, P. (2003). Women's empowerment through home-based work: Evidence from India. *Development and Change, 34*(3), 425–445.

Kirby, M. (1999). Gender and inequality. In M. Kirby (Ed.), *Stratification and differentiation* (pp. 97–117). London: Macmillan Education.

Kishor, S. (1997). *Empowerment of women in Egypt and links to the survival and health of their infants*. Paper presented at the seminar on Female Empowerment and Demographic Processes, Lund.

Klasen, S., & Lamanna, F. (2009). The impact of gender inequality in education and employment on economic growth: New evidence from a panel of countries. *Feminist Economics, 15*(3), 91–132.

Leach, F., & Sitaram, S. (2002). Microfinance and women's empowerment: A lesson from India. *Development in Practice, 12*(5), 575–588.

Longwe, S. H. (1995). Supporting women's development the third world: Distinguishing between intervention and interference. *Gender and Development, 3*(1), 47–50.

Maguire, P. (1984). *Women in development: An alternative analysis.* Amherst, MA: Publications Assistant.

Malhotra, A., & Schuler, S. R. (2005). Women's empowerment as a variable in international development. In D. Narayan (Ed.), *Measuring empowerment: Cross-disciplinary perspectives* (pp. 71–88). Washington,, DC: World Bank.

March, C., Smyth, I. A., & Mukhopadhyay, M. (1999). *A guide to gender-analysis frameworks.* Oxford: Oxfam.

Mason, K. O., & Smith, H. L. (2003). *Women's empowerment and social context: Results from five Asian countries.* Washington, DC: Gender and Development Group, World Bank .

Mayoux, L. (1995). Alternative vision or utopian fantasy? Cooperation, empowerment and women's cooperative development in India. *Journal of International Development, 7*(2), 211–228.

Mininni, G. M. (2014). *Gender and energy issues in the global south: Implications for the post-millennium development goals agenda after 2015.* Constructions of Gender in Research, The Luminary, Lancaster University, UK, no. 5.

Mohideen, R. (2012). *The implications of clean and renewable energy development for gender equality in poor communities in South Asia* (pp. 1–6). Technology and Society in Asia (T&SA), 2012 IEEE Conference on October 27, IEEE.

Momsen, J. (2008). *Women and development in the third world.* London: Routledge.

Momsen, J. H. (2001). *Backlash: Or how to snatch failure from the jaws of success in gender and development.* Thousand Oaks, CA: SAGE.

Momsen, J. H. (2004). *Gender and development.* London: Routledge.

Mosedale, S. (2003). *Towards a framework for assessing empowerment* (pp. 24–25). International Conference, New Directions in Impact Assessment for Development: Methods and Practice, Manchester, November 24 and 25.

Moser, C. (1993). *Gender planning and development: Theory, practice and training.* London: Routledge.

Moser, C. O. (1989). Gender planning in the third world: Meeting practical and strategic gender needs. *World Development, 17*(11), 1799–1825.

Moser, C. O., & Levy, C. (1986). *A theory and methodology of gender planning: Meeting women's practical and strategic needs.* Gender and Planning Working Paper 11. London: Development Planning Unit.

Nagar, R., & Raju, S. (2003). Women, NGOs and the contradictions of empowerment and disempowerment: A conversation. *Antipode, 35*(1), 1–13.

Narayan, D., Chambers, R., Shah, M. K., & Petesch, P. (2000). *Voices of the poor: Crying out for change.* Washington, DC: World Bank.

Nussbaum, M. C. (2001). *Women and human development: The capabilities approach* (Vol. 3). Cambridge: Cambridge University Press.

Oparaocha, S., & Dutta, S. (2011). Gender and energy for sustainable development. *Current Opinion in Environmental Sustainability, 3*(4), 265–271.

O'Reilly, K. (2006). 'Traditional' women, 'modern' water: Linking gender and commodification in Rajasthan, India. *Geoforum, 37*(6), 958–972.

Pankaj, A., & Tankha, R. (2010). Empowerment effects of the NREGS on women workers: a study in four states. *Economic and Political Weekly, 45*(30), 45–55.

Planning Commission Government of India (PCGI) (2002). *Rajasthan development report.* New Delhi: Academic Foundation.

Practical Action. (2013). *Poor people's energy outlook.* Rugby: Practical Action.

Quisumbing, A. R., & Maluccio, J. A. (2003). Resources at marriage and intrahousehold allocation: Evidence from Bangladesh, Ethiopia, Indonesia, and South Africa. *Oxford Bulletin of Economics and Statistics, 65*(3), 283–327.

Rathgeber, E. M. (1990). WID, WAD, GAD: Trends in research and practice. *The Journal of Developing Areas, 24*(4), 489–502.

Ridgeway, C. L. (2011). *Framed by gender: How gender inequality persists in the modern world*. Oxford: Oxford University Press.

Rocheleau, D. E. (2008). Political ecology in the key of policy: From chains of explanation to webs of relation. *Geoforum, 39*(2), 716–727.

Rocheleau, D., Thomas-Slayter, B., & Wangari, E. (1996). *Feminist political ecology: Global issues and local experience*. London and New York: Routledge.

Rojas, A. V., Schmitt, F. M., & Aguilar, L. (2012). *Guidelines on renewable Energy Technologies for Women in Rural and Informal Urban Areas*. IUCN, ENERGIA.

Rowlands, J. (1997). *Questioning empowerment: Working with women in Honduras*. Oxford: Oxfam.

Roy, B. (2011). *Women Barefoot Solar Engineers. A community solution*. Interactive expert Panel. Key policy initiatives and capacity-building on gender mainstreaming: Focus on science and technology. New York, NY: UNCCSW.

Ruiz Abril, M. E. (2009). *Women's economic empowerment in conflict and post-conflict countries. Women's economic empowerment series. SIDA policy, May*. Stockholm: SIDA.

Safa, H. I. (1995). Economic restructuring and gender subordination. *Latin American Perspectives, 22*(2), 32–50.

Santos, F. M. (2012). A positive theory of social entrepreneurship. *Journal of Business Ethics, 111*(3), 335–351.

Schroeder, R. A. (1999). *Shady practices: Agroforestry and gender politics in the Gambia* (Vol. 5). Berkeley: University of California Press.

Schuler, M. (1986). *Empowerment and the law: Strategies of third world women*. Washington, DC: OEF International.

Schuler, M., & Kadirgamar-Rajasingham, S. (1992). Legal literacy: A tool for women's empowerment. In M. Schuler & S. Kadirgamar-Rajasingham (Eds.), *Legal literacy: A tool for women's empowerment* (pp. 21–69). New York, NY: United Nations Development Fund for Women [UNIFEM].

Sen, A. (2001). The many faces of gender inequality. *New Republic, 225*(12), 466–477.

Sen, G. (1997). Empowerment as an Approach to Poverty, Human Development Report, Background Paper, UNDP, 1997. In *BRAC, ICDDRB, Joint Research Project Working Paper No 28(1), New York*.

Sen, G., & Batliwala, S. (2000). Empowering women for reproductive rights. In H. Presser & G. Sen (Eds.), *Women's empowerment and demographic process. Moving beyond Cairo* (pp. 15–36). Oxford: Oxford University Press.

Sharp, J., Briggs, J., Yacoub, H., & Hamed, N. (2003). Doing gender and development: Understanding empowerment and local gender relations. *Transactions of the Institute of British Geographers, 28*(3), 281–295.

Singh, P., & Kumud, D. (2013). Gender disparities among districts of Rajasthan. *International Journal of Innovative Research in Science, Engineering and Technology, 2*(10), 5330–5332.

Skutsch, M. M. (2005). Gender analysis for energy projects and programmes. *Energy for Sustainable Development, 9*(1), 37–52.

Srivastava, N., & Srivastava, R. (2010). Women, work, and employment outcomes in rural India. *Economic and Political Weekly, 45*(28), 49–63.

Stromquist, N. P. (1999). The theoretical and practical basis for empowerment. Women, Education, and Empowerment: Pathways Towards Autonomy. In D. P. Rao & D. P. Latha (Eds.), *Women, education and empowerment* (Vol. 2, pp. 13–22). New Delhi: Discovery Publishing House.

Sundberg, J. (in press). Feminist political ecology. Forthcoming In Douglas Richardson (Ed.), *The international encyclopedia of geography*. Wiley-Blackwell & Association of American Geographers. Retrieved from http://www.academia.edu/14495915/Feminist_Political_Ecology.

Tandon, S. L., & Sharma, R. (2006). Female foeticide and infanticide in India: An analysis of crimes against girl children. *International Journal of Criminal Justice Sciences, 1*(1), 1–10.

United Nations Development Programme (UNDP). (2016). *Sustainable development goals*. Retrieved from http://www.undp.org/content/undp/en/home/sustainable-development-goals/goal-5-gender-equality.html.

Unterhalter, E. (2005). Global inequality, capabilities, social justice: The millennium development goal for gender equality in education. *International Journal of Educational Development, 25*(2), 111–122.

Vinkenburg, C. J. (2015). Beyond the rhetoric of choice: Promoting women's economic empowerment in developed countries. *IDS Bulletin, 46*(4), 28–32.

Williams, J. (2005). *Measuring gender and women's empowerment using confirmatory factor analysis.* Boulder, CO: Population Program, Institute of Behavioural Science, University of Colorado.

Yin, R. K. (2011). *Applications of case study research.* London: Sage.

Yin, R. K. (2015). *Qualitative research from start to finish.* Guilford: Guilford Press.

Protecting Indonesia's women migrant workers from the grassroots: a story of Paguyuban Seruni*

Elisabeth Dewi and Sylvia Yazid

ABSTRACT

This paper was written based on a research at the grassroots level which was aimed to look into: (1) the relative position of women *vis-a-vis* the process of making policies on the protection of women migrant workers; (2) what efforts women have made; (3) what efforts women can potentially make, based on their current positions; and (4) opportunities and challenges that may arise. In arguing for the importance of women's empowerment in conducting protection efforts for Indonesian women migrant workers, the research made the activities of three women activists from Paguyuban Seruni in Banyumas, Indonesia the object of analysis. The efforts and roles were identified through in-depth interviews and observations. Through self-development, enriching process and optimal achievement, along with access to education and involvement in the democratization process at the grassroots level, the women activists have made a valuable contribution to the efforts of protecting women migrant workers at the grassroots level. There are limitations and problems that these women have to face, but they all become motivations for them to move forward and actually do something through a process where self and community achievement are interrelated. At this stage of the research, this paper is aimed to showcase the lessons learned and best practices identified from the grassroots level, in the search for efforts worth making, developing and duplicating, with the aim of protecting women migrant workers working in the informal sector.

Introduction

This paper is related to two main issues. The first issue is about Indonesian women who are working abroad in informal and domestic sectors, who mainly work as domestic workers. According to the International Labor Organization (ILO, 2016), until 2013, among 150.3 million migrant workers in the whole world, 66.6 million or 55.7% of them are women. It is also noted that 11.5 million of them are domestic workers. Besides this, according

---

*This article was written based on the data gathered during a research funded by LPPM UNPAR in the year 2015 with the title of 'Identifikasi Potensi Perempuan di Akar Rumput dalam Upaya Perlindungan Buruh Migran Perempuan Indonesia,' conducted by Elisabeth Dewi and Sylvia Yazid.

to the data from *Badan Nasional Penempatan dan Perlindungan Tenaga Kerja Indonesia (BNP2TKI)*, or the National Authority for the Placement and Protection of Indonesian Overseas Workers, for the year 2011–2016, among the total of 2,603,683 workers who were served by BNP2TKI to work abroad, 1,529,669 or around 58.75% are women (BNP2TKI, 2016). There are not any official records which provide the exact number of Indonesian workers working as domestic workers abroad; however, the data from BNP2TKI also show that housemaids, nannies and caregivers are common jobs of Indonesian women workers abroad. These kinds of jobs are temporary, contract-based and informal, which differentiate Indonesian women and men workers. Moreover, the fact that they are working in houses which are isolated from the outside world, as they are considered private spaces, often makes these women workers vulnerable to tortures and abuses. However, this condition is not sufficiently regulated in the policies, laws and regulations for workers, both from the sending country and the host country.

A continuously growing attention to the feminization of migrant workers is due to several factors such as (1) a vast increase in the number of women working outside their country; (2) the micro and macro-economic significance of the remittances they bring to their country of origin; and (3) the problematic characteristics of their work, especially for those who are working in the informal sector.[1] Even though unpaid salary and undocumented[2] status could happen to both men migrant workers who work in plantations, construction sites or factories, and to women who work as domestic workers, the conditions of domestic workers tend to be worse because of torture and containment. A number of researchers (Ball & Piper, 2006; Chant, 1992; Loveband, 2006; Yamanaka & Piper, 2005; Young, 2006) have made the feminization of migrant workers as the focus or the main element of their papers. However, in most of their studies, women are portrayed as the 'victims' of the misconducts during the process of migration as workers. This paper departs from the main idea that it is important to see women not only as 'passive actors' in the context of labor migration.

The second highlighted issue is the potential of a number of women at the grassroots level, who come from various local communities at the origin areas, to conduct activities to prevent or solve issues experienced by women migrant workers. Women at the grassroots level become a very important subject because of their close position to, and involvement in, women migrant workers' daily lives. This paper aims to look into: (1) the relative position of women *vis-a-vis* the process of making policies on the protection of women migrant workers; (2) what efforts they have made; (3) what efforts they potentially make based on their current positions; and (4) opportunities and challenges that may arise. This paper is expected to document the efforts worth making to provide better protections for Indonesian migrant workers in the informal sector.

A number of papers have analyzed the topic of temporary Asian migrant workers comprehensively, and continue to create documentation on how the process of migrant workers is not working, especially for women (Anggraeni, 2006; Chin, 2002; Dewi, 2010; HRW, 2004; Hugo, 2005; Jones, 2000; Kaur, 2007; Komnas & Solidaritas, 2002, 2003; Pigay, 2005; Yazid, 2013). As has been highlighted by Young and Chant, compared to men, women migrant workers have more limited access to work because most of them do not have adequate skills or are even unskilled. This condition has limited their work options to low status and low paid jobs in informal and hospitality sectors. In most cases, they are forced to do the so-called 3Ds jobs (dirty, degrading and dangerous), which is temporary and short-contracted.

The focus on the identification of womens' positions and what they have done and they might do in this research is inspired by Enloe's work (2000), *Bananas, beaches and bases: Making feminist sense of international politics*. One of the most important arguments from this work is that to understand international politics more comprehensively, we need to pay attention to different instances experienced by women. For example, in the case of trafficking of women, Enloe argues that in order to get better understanding about the international system, we need to find answers to questions why women are trafficked, who gets the benefits and who closes their eyes toward the abuse that has been occurring. In the case of women migrant workers, it is assumed that questions like why those women decided to migrate, what kind of abuses that they experience and why are they abused has been explained in the existing literature. Therefore, this research aims to picture Indonesian women migrant workers through Enloe's description of 'beyond the global victim.' Analyzing the efforts made by women at the grassroots level and identifying their potentials will provide profound understanding on the issue of women migrant workers and contributes to the enhancement of the protection of Indonesian migrant workers.

In regards to the topic of domestic workers, Enloe underlines that international political debt which occurred in the end of 1990s put pressure the governments with debts to adopt policies that cut the budget for social service for the sake of paying their debts. This kind of policy influenced women and men differently and in most cases, women as the 'manager' of the family are disadvantaged. Moreover, in the condition where lack of job vacancies occurs, women are also expected to find income, the role which is traditionally played by men in Asian culture. Therefore, to end this condition or at least to minimize the possibility of the condition being worsened, women need to be actively involved in the process of policy-making, implementation and monitoring.

Previous research conducted by Sylvia Yazid and published in 2013 has elaborated on the efforts made by Non-Governmental Organizations (NGOs) in influencing domestic and foreign policies on the placement and protection of Indonesian workers abroad. It has shown that the efforts to promote a policy that can provide better protection for Indonesian workers, particularly women, have been initiated since quite a long time. The reformation in Indonesia clearly has made changes to the involvement of NGOs in the policy-making and implementation processes. That research has also shown that the domestic policy-making process tends to be more open to the involvement of non-governmental stakeholders. Meanwhile, the foreign policy-making process is more closed. The research conducted by Elisabeth Dewi in West Java and Central Java has successfully identified several working situations experienced by women migrant workers in Saudi Arabia and Malaysia. Those working situations generated several challenges which are often related specifically to the feminization of those migrant workers. For instance, the research shows that there are not any social policies that support women migrant workers to do their role as a mother, a wife and a member of community where they come from. In-depth interview sessions with the women migrant workers and their relatives showed that there are not any optimal situations that relate to the process of empowerment, investment and enhancement of their capability as women. These two pieces of research have further highlighted the need to identify women's potential at the grassroots level to contribute to the policy-making process. Sylvia Yazid and Elisabeth Dewi (2015) have published the first part of a research on the potentials of women in improving the protection of Indonesian women migrant workers in the work titled 'Women on the steering wheel: Identifying the potentials of women in improving the protection of Indonesian women migrant workers' (Yazid & Dewi, 2015). This work focused more on the potential of women at the national level in influencing Indonesian policies on migrant workers and improving the protection of Indonesian women migrant workers. This article, complementing the previous one, focuses more on the women at the grassroots level. It takes the form of telling the story of three women activists from an area of origin, who share some similar experiences as former migrant workers and also differences as they choose their own paths in their lives. The subjectivity of each woman is highlighted, as well as their collective visions and actions.

Methodology

This research focused on the experience of three former women migrant workers, Narsidah, Lili Purwani and Sri Setiawati, who are members of Paguyuban Peduli Buruh Migran dan Perempuan Seruni, Association Concerning Migrant Workers and Women Seruni[3] in the sub-district of Sumbang, regency of Banyumas. They are chosen for the following reasons: First, this research aims to highlight efforts made by the women who are usually seen as the 'victim.' These three women are former women migrant workers, who during their migration process experienced problems commonly faced by women migrant workers such as unpaid salaries, undocumented status and even family or marital issues. Second, the research aims to document lessons learned by the former women migrant workers from the efforts to overcome their problems and empower themselves. The three women, to a certain degree, have managed to overcome their problems and in the process of empowering themselves through their works. Third, this research also wants to observe how while helping and empowering themselves, the former women migrant workers are also helping and empowering other women migrant workers around them. The three women are now living and working in towns in Central Java, which are the areas of origin for significant number of women migrant workers, many of which are continuous ones. It is assumed that their efforts have the potential to influence other women.

These three women were interviewed to obtain their story and to understand how they perceive their efforts and the results. It was continued with an observation of how they work and interact with other stakeholders through the activity called Information Training for Indonesian Migrant Workers with the title of 'Mewujudkan Perlindungan dan Pemberdayaan TKI/BMI sejak dari Hulu' or 'Protection and Empowerment for Indonesian Migrant Workers from the Top' in Gumelar village, regency of Banyumas. At this occasion, we also interviewed a number of stakeholders that have worked with the three women, including a local leader, a government representative, a facilitator from another NGO and a volunteer, in an effort to confirm the information obtained from the three women.

The efforts of empowering women migrant workers: stories from the grassroots

Narsidah, the founder[4]
Narsidah used to be a migrant worker in Singapore in 1998. Her decision to work in Singapore as a migrant worker was due to the economic crisis that made her former company

decide to lay off some workers. She decided to follow the steps of her first sibling to be a migrant worker. She lived in an agency for two months before being sent to Singapore. During her first time working as a migrant worker abroad, Narsidah felt uncomfortable and always wanted to go back to Indonesia. She only managed to work for a year and two months before she went back home with her own money because she did not want to work in Singapore anymore.

When she arrived in Indonesia, she did not know what kind of work she had to do; therefore, she decided to become a migrant worker again. She was also sponsored to go to Taiwan. As a mother with one child, she had been through so many experiences that made her will to establish an organization once she could go home. She wanted to establish an organization that works to organize migrant workers, conduct activities so people can learn together, and help other migrant workers and their family who are facing problems.

Inhuman conditions happened in the shelter, and lack of facilities and a lack of water made the migrant worker candidates have to line up from three in the morning to take a shower. The minimal bedroom facilities also led to fights between migrant worker candidates. The provided food was only a piece of cassava in the morning, or only vegetables and salted fish. Moreover, Narsidah found out that some of her friends in the shelter have already been in the shelter for more than one year and still not departed to the destination country. Looking at these facts, Narsidah saw the need to report her opinions to the owner of the agency. Then Narsidah encouraged some of her friends in the shelter to demand for improvements of their current living condition to the owner of the company.

On the second day, Narsidah and her friends were detained by the security when they were conducting a discussion. Approximately, 300 migrant worker candidates were detained and locked inside a room. They tried to throw papers outside the room and hoped that someone would help and call the police or any NGOs. Finally, they found a way out by burning the lock at the exit door and they managed to escape from the security. A few hours later, an NGO managed to evacuate them. With the help of NGOs and the current Minister of Women Development, Khofifah Indar Parawansa, the victims were placed in a shelter and were facilitated for a few days.

Narsidah still wanted to become a migrant worker; however, this time she did not go to Taiwan, but to Hong Kong. After talking to several staff as well as migrant workers who are working in Hong Kong, Narsidah went to the agency without having a sponsor. A few agencies rejected her because she did not have any sponsor for her departure to Hong Kong. Eventually, she could find an agency who accepted her even though she did not have a sponsor. As it turned out, she was treated differently to other migrant workers who are sponsored. She was always being watched and kept away from the other migrant worker candidates. She was also frequently invited to go out with the company staff or often asked to accompany the director's wife, so she did not have much time to train to prepare for her departure. During the interview, she was criticized that she did not have adequate language skills to be able to go to Hong Kong and for other reasons. From that moment, she refused any invitation to go out and chose to focus on her training. Her decision to focus on training and her privileges to go out every weekend made the other migrant workers jealous. She was terrorized by the senior migrant workers and was told to sleep near the door so she could be watched easily. She actually realized that it was unfair if only she was allowed to go out at the weekend, so she decided to recommend to the director to give free days on the weekend to the other migrant workers. The director of the agency agreed, so every weekend the migrant workers were freed from training activities and were allowed to leave the agency for personal activities. However, this condition led to negative impacts because there were some migrant workers who ran away or got pregnant.

Narsidah's activeness in the agency delayed her departure for six months until finally she was able to go to Hong Kong. Even though she got a simple job, which was to take care of the elderly, her rights were not fulfilled and she was only given half of the promised salary. The migrant workers in Hong Kong told her that there is a law saying that Sunday is a free day for them; however, Narsidah's employer did not care about it so her salary was cut every time she went out on Sunday to meet her organization friends. Because of this unfairness, she reported her boss which resulted in a staff member from the agency in Jakarta going to Hong Kong to meet her. The staff put the blame on her for going out on Sunday to meet her organization friends, and did not defend her right to get a free day every Sunday.

Narsidah then requested to have a new employer because her rights were not being fulfilled by her previous employer, and the person whom she need to take care of died. With her last employer, she was also not treated well, due to the fact that her employer was bankrupt so she was not paid for three months. However, that issue was being settled well through mediation. During her stay in Hong Kong, she was active in the Indonesian Migrant Worker Union (IMWU), which is the only migrant organization that is acknowledged by the government of Hong Kong. In that organization, Narsidah focused on advocating cases, conducting training and setting up educational events for migrant workers in Hong Kong.

After returning from Hong Kong, she decided to take Paket C[5] to get a certificate so she could continue her dream to study and establish an organization. In her spare time, she used her time to handle existing migrant workers' cases. Narsidah and her friends from Seruni were also thinking about how to share the work with the Office of Manpower in handling the cases, because not all cases could be handled by Seruni due to the lack of manpower and available capital.

Narsidah also urged women migrant workers candidates to be well prepared. Even though they will only work as domestic workers, they have to prepare and plan everything well and have a target and a wish for the future. Therefore, by being a migrant worker, women will not only see the materials that they will receive but also utilize their time to obtain knowledge and skills. For the migrant workers who are currently doing their job, Narsidah advised them to rethink and determine their wish before their departure, so they will not waste their time and they could achieve so many things by preparing themselves for after returning to Indonesia. According to her, becoming a migrant worker is not a main dream, but a stepping stone as a platform to learn. Even though becoming a migrant worker is not considered as a good thing to do because of the stigma, the migrant workers could prove themselves or set a good example, like some of Narsidah friends who went as migrant workers and then returned to Indonesia with a degree, or established a startup business in their areas.

Seruni was established at the end of 2008. After Narsidah returned from Hong Kong, most of her activities were assisting her friends from other organizations outside Banyumas. Then, she had an idea to gather some friends and establish an organization in

Banyumas. Starting by collecting some information about actors who are concerned about the issue of women and migrants, she went to see them one by one to discuss and to ask for help. She eventually received a lot of support from friends and academics, members of Regional House of Representative (Dewan Perwakilan Rakyat Daerah or DPRD) and activists. Seruni was established, despite the doubts from the Office of Manpower on the idea to create an organization for migrant workers. Narsidah faced a number of challenges. Some of Seruni's earlier members decided to go abroad again to work again. Also, Narsidah had to use money from her own pocket in conducting case advocacy. Nevertheless, Seruni survived by learning from the lawyers on how to follow up cases that have been reported to the government officials. Understanding the authorities of the Office of Manpower and DPRD also helped Narsidah in determining what cases to handle and how. Seruni began to understand why there are not any significant changes after all the hard work they have done. Initially, the relationship between Seruni and the department of manpower was disharmonious. To improve this condition, Narsidah decided to come more often to the department, not only to talk about cases but also to do small talks. From these encounters, she got the information that there is not any budget to handle migrant workers' cases in Banyumas.

Narsidah received a lot of assistance from the DPRD of Banyumas. The *Commission D*[6] of the DPRD proposed the allocation of a budget for handling cases of migrant workers that keep on happening in Banyumas at the DPRD's general meeting (*Paripurna*).[7] Narsidah argued that the commitment of Seruni members is not enough; the parliament members also need to understand how to allocate the given budget. In 2001, IDR 60,000,000 was allocated to handle the cases of migrant workers as well as to do socialization and preventive actions. In 2012, the budget was raised to IDR 150,000,000; however, the budget allocation and the understanding of parliament members are only limited to problem solving. Thus, the budget can only be used to handle the cases, while socialization activities like safe migration training and other preventive efforts could not use the budget from the government.

Besides handling cases, Seruni is also involved in reviewing policies and influencing the policy-making process. Seruni tried to influence the local government's policy by asking for the commitment of the elected *Bupati* (head of regency) who was campaigning to make a local regulation to protect the migrant workers. Seruni was then contacted to discuss the local regulation about protection of migrant workers that will be implemented. Seruni also urged for the implementation of local regulation as an effort to protect migrant workers, considering that Banyumas is the fourth biggest city within Central Java province that sends approximately 2000 migrant workers abroad every year. The local regulation was eventually enforced in 2015. Seruni also encouraged the involvement of related institutions. An example of the result of Seruni's effort is how public offices like *Badan Pemberdayaan Masyarakat*, the agency of community development, now have programs related to migrant workers.

The greater support for civil society involvement from local parliament members and leaders has become more common in local levels in Indonesia. With Indonesia's decentralization policy, these executive and legislative branches at the local level are given more power to organize themselves. Realizing that they do not have adequate experience, knowledge and capability to do so, many of them are opening up the policy process, including to civil society organizations like Seruni. While the policy-makers gain inputs and assistance in the policy-making, the civil society organizations have the opportunity to direct the policies in a preferable direction, in this case to protect women migrant workers.

The main challenge which Narsidah faced in Seruni is the lack of human resources and the slow process of regeneration, because Seruni was established by the community, based on personal willingness to help the migrant workers. Initially, many wanted to become staff and help Seruni, but because of other activities like having a family, and working again as migrant workers, their contribution to Seruni became not optimal. One of Narsidah's friends who graduated from the University of Indonesia preferred to work in a bank rather than to come back to Banyumas and become a staff member in Seruni. These kinds of instances are explained by Narsidah as the causes of Seruni's lack of human resources and financial support. As understood by Narsidah, this is due to the fact that Seruni is a social movement and established as a platform to learn together, with no binding regulation. The low availability of resources and capital also makes Seruni's activities become limited. However, Narsidah and her friends in Seruni keep on trying to help the migrant workers.

The future opportunities for Narsidah and friends in Seruni are to invite new people to join the organization. She believes that through organization, they could support one another, especially in Seruni, which works within migrant workers' environments and aims to create shared sentiments among members. There are only a limited number of migrants based in Banyumas which could be handled by Seruni. A lot of *kepala desa* (heads of village), and *camat* (heads of sub-district), asked Seruni to give socialization and training for the residents; however, because of the lack of manpower and financial support, Narsidah could not fulfill the requests.

The lack of capacity in handling cases and the unfulfilled rights of migrant workers made Narsidah and her fellow staff of Seruni wish to have a lawyer who specifically works on the issue of migrant workers. Therefore, they support each other to study at university. Narsidah decided to take turns with the other staff in continuing their study so Seruni's activities could still be conducted. Narsidah let Lili to study at the university first. With the financial support from the parliament members and some stakeholders who have been cooperating with Seruni, in 2011, Lili began her study in the Faculty of Law of the Jenderal Soedirman University. The following year, Narsidah got the chance to study in the Faculty of Law of the University of Wijayakusuma Purwokerto with the financial support given from the Diocese of Purwokerto. Narsidah successfully completed her study with a final paper on the problems related to migrant workers' placement contracts. Narsidah is continuing her study to become a legal advocate with the financial support from a local law activist.

Lili Purwani, the partner[8]

Lili is an activist of Paguyuban Seruni in the region of Datar village, Banyumas, Central Java. She was the head of Paguyuban Seruni several times. Besides helping Seruni, she was also doing her final project for her study at the Faculty of Law in the Soedirman University. The chosen topic for her final project or her thesis is about migrant workers' issues, specifically those related to the role of the department of manpower in protecting Indonesian workers. Before studying at university, she went to a Vocational High School majoring in hospitality.

Besides conducting case advocacy, Lili and her friends also tried to influence local government policies. An example is the ratification of a local government regulation (Perda) No. 2 in 2012 about the protection for migrant workers in Banyumas which was the promise of the Bupati of Banyumas during his campaign. Besides being a catalyst in influencing the policy, Lili also did some empowerment efforts, including economic ones, for the former migrant workers in the region of Banyumas. The efforts to empower them were conducted through training to create mats from patchwork, training related to fishing and livestock industry and also training on culinary art. The empowerment effort is then followed by assistance in marketing the products. The patchwork mats are marketed to several stores or household sections in department stores. Lili also conducted a program for left behind children[9] which was conducted for six months, and also a program that provides an internet house for migrant workers, which was conducted for a year. However, Lili was disappointed because those programs were only conducted once. This is due to the fact that implementation of those programs was limited by the budget given from external sectors and the regency. Obviously, sustainability is an issue for them.

There are several challenges that were faced by Lili. The first challenge that was faced by Lili and Paguyuban Seruni was the limited budget for operational purposes and financing the programs that they have planned. The second challenge, as stated by Narsidah, was related to human resources and regeneration. It is difficult for them to find someone who is willing and capable to continue the vision and mission of Paguyuban Seruni. Lili believes that this has a lot to do with the fact that Lili's profession or what she does is not based on how much money a person could get, but how much willingness a person has. Besides the internal challenges, Lili was also faced with external challenges. For example, PPTKIS (Perusahaan Pengerah Tenaga Kerja Indonesia Swasta), the Private Placement Agency of Indonesian Workers, has become their opposition in handling an issue of intimidating PJTKI, the Indonesian Labor Providers Organization.

Lili was a migrant worker who worked in Hong Kong for seven months. She was a victim of one-sided termination of employment from her employer. Lili became a migrant worker in September 2002 and returned to Indonesia in April 2003. She was a migrant worker from Datar village, Banyumas, Central Java. Before becoming a migrant worker in Hong Kong, she lived in the shelter for four months. At the beginning, before joining and establishing Seruni, she met her NGO colleagues and Narsidah who had worked in Hong Kong, in Jakarta. She also lived in Jakarta for almost a year where she learned various things with Narsidah and her NGO colleagues. Finally, after almost a year, she decided to go back to Datar village in Banyumas to establish Paguyuban Seruni and to help in solving migrant worker issues in her village.

Lili hopes to continue to fight for Paguyuban Seruni. She believes that the next generation is needed to continue the fight for handling migrant worker issues because there are still many migrant workers issues which are not tackled until this moment. Lili has a hope to make migrant workers candidates receive valid, complete and correct information so they can migrate safely. She also believes that a carefully planned salary management is needed for the migration to be beneficial.

Sri Setyawati, the educator[10]
Sri Setyawati or Sri is one of the activists in Paguyuban Seruni, who focuses her activities in Gumelar area, Banyumas, Central Java. In the area of Gumelar, Sri specifically works in

Panikaben village. Gumelar is also one of the biggest areas of origin for migrant workers in Central Java. Sri is 41 years old, a wife and a mother to three children. Her first child is studying in Semarang majoring Health Environment. Her second child is studying in her 12th grade and her third child is studying in the 2nd grade. Sri herself only graduated from Junior High School, but after returning to Indonesia and decided not to become a migrant worker anymore, she did the Paket C. After completing Paket C, she continued to study in early childhood education and currently she is in her sixth semester.

Sri has been managing PAUD (playgroup) since 2009 until now. The PAUD Jatiwaluyo in Panikaben village has 37 students with 5 teachers, 3 of them are former migrant workers. Every teacher is encouraged to continue their studies to the university level. Four of them are studying in the university and one is doing the Paket C. During the first two years, students are not obliged to pay fees. On the third year, they have to pay IDR 5000, and every year the fee raises ||IDR 2500 and now the fee is IDR 15,000. In the year 2014, PAUD got a financial help because Sri was active in PNPM, a Nationwide Community Program. PNPM assistances enabled Sri to build a building for the PAUD on a land she personally own. On 10 February 2015, Sri was involved in the district association of PAUD.

Sri has three activities in Seruni Gumelar: first, the *Bina Keluarga TKI*, a program for the family of migrant workers. In Gumelar, specifically in Panikaben village, there are a number of former migrant workers that can reach 400 people. Sri is trying to convince the former migrant workers not to go abroad again and giving them knowledge about what is going to be received after their return. Other activity that is conducted is the education on how to raise children for the husbands whose wives are working as migrant workers.

Second, related to advocacy. There are a lot of issues that happen to former migrant workers that Lili helps advocating. For instance, getting the migrant workers' deposits back from agencies which went bankrupt. There are also migrant workers who could not go home to their home country. Many of these cases settled already.

Third, related to economic empowerment. As explained before, the economic empowerment was done through patchwork mats making facilitated by Seruni and the Soedirman University. Sri worked really hard in searching for the materials and conducting the marketing process. Unfortunately, the motivation of the former migrant workers is only limited to getting paid from this economic empowerment program. Meanwhile, Sri hopes that from this activity the former migrant workers could learn how to be involved in an organization. Furthermore, there is a lack of human resources that have the ability to work on the designs, making it difficult for innovations.

There are three main challenges faced by Sri as an activist in Paguyuban Seruni. First, related to regeneration; every time there was an activity in the district, there would be no people who would attend the activity if Sri could not join. They tend to follow the lead. There is no sense of ownership among them. They tend to receive assistance rather than to be involved or to contribute. Second, challenges are related to the marketing of the product from the economic empowerment. Sri is confident that she can still handle issues related to production, but not those related to the marketing process. At the beginning, when there are only a small number of producer who make mats from patchwork, it was easier to sell them. When there are a lot of mat producers in the neighborhood, the demand for the product decreased. The effort to do the marketing outside Gumelar region has been done; however, they still face challenges. Third, as in other cases, they face challenges in terms of financial support. Up to this moment, the financial support comes from Sri's own pocket.

Sri became a migrant worker for the first time in 1999. Her first destination country was Taiwan. She worked there for five years. Her first contract was in 1999 and then she went home in 2001. She went abroad again in 2002, and she returned in 2005. When she returned, she opened a small store; however at the end, she lost her interest. Later on, Sri took part in some meetings, until finally she become active in PKK, a program to educate women and improve their family welfare, which led her to establish PAUD.

Sri hopes that her migrant worker colleagues have strong motivation to develop their potential in their hometown. The salary gap between what is received in Indonesia and abroad is huge; however, it is important to have a strong base and a strong willingness to work for their own country, so they could help other former migrant workers. Further-more, for the migrant workers who are still working abroad, Sri hopes that they could be more active in Indonesian migrant worker organizations or writing their stories to be published.

Protecting through empowerment

The profiling of the three women activists from Paguyuban Seruni above explained directly and concisely that the protection of Indonesian migrant workers is needed to be initiated from the empowerment of women who are involved in the process. It should be realized that without empowerment, a protection effort would be pointless. Narsidah, Lili and Sri are the examples of women individuals who successfully managed to promote the concept of empowerment through their experiences, family and commu-nity. The following is an analysis of three main dimensions that are related to each other that influence the process of empowerment: resources, agency and achievements. In this research, the agency dimension is understood through a discussion about the process. Those three dimensions are related to each other and influenced the process of social change which becomes a motivation of empowerment, with this following scheme as Kabeer (1999b) points out:

| **resources** | **agency** | **achievements** |
| (pre-conditions) | (process) | (outcomes) |

Resources

In accordance with Kabeer's (1999b) explanation, resources are not an abstract concept but a dynamic concept and could be a movement mediator from a form of power to another form of power. This power is later distributed through several institutions and relations among societies. By looking at that explanation, these three activists from Paguyuban Seruni use their acquired positions to strengthen several decision-making pro-cesses, both internally and externally, which are related to the protection of migrant workers in their working environment. By increasing their ability, individually and institu-tionally, they can influence the authorities to find priority in policy-making at the grass-roots level, sub-district and even the higher level like regency.

Agency

These women conducted several activities, both individually and collectively, showing their commitment toward the protection of the migrant workers in their working environment. They stated that their life choices are to be directly involved in a series of power achievement which is called as power within. They learn to do a series of negotiation processes, bargaining processes and even protests, to reach more beneficial position for the community that they represent and the migrant workers in several processes of decision-making about their life. In accordance with the explanation from Kabeer (1999b), the process that they are going through is based on the means, motivation and the purpose that they have in their daily life as a part of the community or 'paguyuban.' Through the explanations from the three activists from Seruni, we can see that the process is usually influenced by several conditions that hamper the institution or the community or 'paguyuban,' specifically related to the issue of regeneration. This disability could lead to a decrease of their ability to make strategic choices in their life. This issue, in the long term, could make a change in a way how they look at themselves and their capacity to empower themselves and the surrounding community.

Achievement

Explanations on resources possessed and process experienced by the three activists from Paguyuban Seruni showed their abilities and potential that contributed to their condition as it is today. They have enough awareness to state what they have achieved and what they still want to do, both individually and together with the community. Narsidah, Lili and Sri are the women who have willingness and ability to free themselves and become the ones who are more independent, so they do not need to depend on other people to continue living their life.

From these three women, we could see a relation between resources, process and achievement in a very active form. Actively and continually, they increase their own capacity, as in resources, to be able to increase their life process as individual and as a part of community. Through several activities, they question and reevaluate their role and responsibility to be able to make changes in protecting the Indonesian migrant workers, which relate to the current condition and situation.

Kabeer (1999a) explains that the three above-mentioned dimensions, resources, process and achievement, have to be seen as a flow that influence one another. A change in one dimension will influence the other dimension. Instances in the achievement dimension could influence the other dimensions in the future. In these three following women activists, we could see their achievements which are based on their awareness to get access to higher education as an effort to empower themselves and to be able to protect other migrant workers.

Educational access

These three activists from Paguyuban Seruni have proven that access to education will lead to women's empowerment. Narsidah and Lili are already committed with all their heart to obtaining the bachelor's degree in the Faculty of Law to be able to assist migrant workers with the law at various levels. Narsidah believes that by getting herself educated to become a legal advocate will make her able to solve more difficult legal problems at higher levels. Moreover, Sri, amid her packed activities as an activist and a mother to two children, has committed to work in the sector of early childhood education to fulfill her dream, which is to create better generation in the future.

In accordance with the argument put forward by Kabeer (1999a), there are several changes that are caused by their education that has been experienced by the three activists from Paguyuban Seruni, which are:

1. Education has influenced the way of thinking and the behavior of those three activists. They, who come from marginalized community, who are former migrant workers from small and poor villages, managed to improve their life process to gain power in doing a number of efforts to protect other migrant workers who are coming from similar communities.
2. Education has widened the opportunity for them to get access to knowledge, information and new ideas. Through wider contacts with the outer world, outside their family and community, they have more ability to use those abilities effectively in the process of assisting and protecting migrant workers, especially the migrant worker candidates who are younger and less experienced.
3. Education has increased their life quality both individually and through the community in accordance with the choices that they took.
4. Education has brought impacts that are related to the power that they have inside and outside of their own life. In this case, education has allowed these women more important roles in the decision-making process. Furthermore, education has enabled these women to redefine men's domination in their household and their community. In short, these women are able to have a higher bargaining position. Up to this moment, Lili still chooses to be single, while Narsidah decided to become a single parent for her only child after getting a divorce from her husband. Sri and her husband live together with their two children managing their own business.

Collective actions

A series of activities conducted by the three women activists from Paguyuban Seruni and their achievements to push a process of transformation in the protection of migrant workers at various levels is a form of what Kabeer (1999a) calls 'political pressure from the bottom.' The women who have managed to empower themselves, by using different processes, represent a marginal group and fight to defend their rights at various levels.

The efforts that they have made together with official institutions at the village, sub-district and regency/city levels, with university students, academics and NGOs, are the center of where the social transformation occurred, both for them and for Paguyuban Seruni as a part of a bigger community. As a result, a wider opportunity is opened for them to get involved in a wider public arena, which may lead them directly or indirectly in a long term to challenge the patriarchal power in different institutions.

Paguyuban Seruni was not created to be involved politically, but in a form that requires them to work hard for the protection of migrant workers, which is very much related to the process of achieving equality, democratization, empowerment, development and enhancement of the identity of the villagers, especially for the migrant workers and migrant worker candidates. This condition is expected to create a significant push to other women to participate in the development process and the enhancement of welfare in their daily life as a part of the community.

Conclusion and recommendations

This paper has analyzed the efforts made by three women activists at the grassroots level through Paguyuban Seruni which are believed to have contributed to the wider effort to protect Indonesian migrant workers. Through a series of long and uneasy processes, they managed to do actions together, supported by the education that does not only empower themselves, but also the migrant workers whom they assist. Their existence at the grass-roots level with their experience and background as migrant workers strengthened their familiarity with the root causes of migrant worker problems, and the process of empow-erment for the migrant workers they are assisting. Their ability to conduct their activities is also determined by the support they get from other stakeholders such as supporting local leaders and parliament members. This is an increasingly common case in Indonesia, where local parliament members and leaders are involving civil society more in policy-making, implementation and monitoring. This research could still be developed by deepening the research questions with follow-up questions that come up from the analyses to acquire more in-depth answers. The research would also benefit from adding more corre-spondents to cater to other groups of actors, for instance, successful migrant workers and male actors, and widening the focus of research to cater to aspects other than the protec-tion efforts, such as efforts to productively utilize their remittance so that they do not need to work abroad anymore. Therefore, further research with a wider scope is needed, in an attempt to contribute to a broader and more comprehensive protection mechanism for migrant workers.

Notes

1. A study about issues usually faced by Indonesian women migrant workers in their migration steps, before departure, during their work, and after their work abroad can be found in Yazid (2013).
2. Several terms are used to describe migrant workers who have problems with their migration. The common terms which are often used by academics and activists are undocumented or irregular migrants. The term 'illegal migrant workers' is usually used by the government, usually from the destination country. The differences between these terms are related to the different point of views on what caused migration problems and what the impacts toward the status of the migrants are. Those who oppose the use of 'illegal migrant' as a term argue that the workers are not illegal as humans. What happens is at one point of their migration process; they do not have the required documents. However this condition often occurs not because of the migrant workers' fault. There is a possibility that a woman migrant worker who is working as a domestic worker has to run away from her employer who frequently tortures her. However, because the employer keeps her passport, she becomes undocumented.
3. In this paper, the association will be referred as Paguyuban Seruni or Seruni.
4. Interview with Narsidah, in Banyumas, 30 June 2015

5. Paket C is a special short programme for those who did not actually attend high school to obtain a certificate comparable to regular high school certificate.
6. A commission that works on the sector of citizens' welfare.
7. The highest assembly in the House of Representative of Republic of Indonesia, which is led by the head of House of Representative.
8. Interview with Lili Purwani in Banyumas, 30 June 2015
9. Children who are temporarily left behind to stay with their fathers or relatives by their mothers who work abroad.
10. Interview with Sri Setyawati in Banyumas, 1 July 2015

Disclosure statement

No potential conflict of interest was reported by the authors.

References

Anggraeni, D. (2006). *Dreamseekers: Indonesian women as domestic workers in Asia*. Jakarta: Equinox Pub.
Ball, R., & Piper, N. (2006). Trading labour-trading rights: The regional dynamics of rights recognition for migrant workers in the Asia-Pacific. In K. Hewison & K. Young (Eds.), *Transnational migration and work in Asia* (pp. 213–233). Abingdon: Routledge.
BNP2TKI. (2016). *Data Penempatan dan Perlindungan TKI*. Retrieved September 7, 2016, from http://www.bnp2tki.go.id/uploads/data/data_08-08-2016_072751_Laporan_Pengolahan_Data_BNP2TKI_S.D_JULI_2016.pdf.
Chant, S. (1992). Conclusion: Towards a framework for the analysis of gender-selective migration. In S. H. Chant (Ed.), *Gender and migration in developing countries* (pp. 174–196). London: Belhaven Press.
Chin, C. B. N. (2002). The 'host' state and the 'guest' worker in Malaysia: Public management and migrant labour in times of economic prosperity and crisis. *Asia Pacific Business Review, 8*, 19–40.
Dewi, E. (2010). *Relationships between women migrant workers and their children in Indonesia; feminist perspectives, community values and motherhood* (PhD thesis). Victoria University, Australia.
Enloe, C. (2000). *Bananas, beaches and bases: Making feminist sense of international politics*. London: University of California Press.

HRW. (2004). *Help wanted: Abuses against female migrant domestic workers in Indonesia and Malaysia.* Kuala Lumpur: Human Rights Watch.

Hugo, G. (2005). Indonesian international domestic workers: Contemporary developments and issues. In S. Huang, B. S. A. Yeoh, & R. Noor Abdul (Eds.), *Asian women as transnational domestic workers* (pp. 54–91). Singapore: Marshall Cavendish Academic.

ILO. (2016, July 11). *Global estimates on migrant workers, results and methodology: Special focus on migrant domestic workers* [Online]. Retrieved July 11, 2016, from http://www.ilo.org/wcmsp5/groups/public/---dgreports/---dcomm/documents/publication/wcms_436343.pdf.

Jones, S. (2000). *Making money off migrants: The Indonesian exodus to Malaysia.* Hong Kong Wollongong, NSW.: Capstrans, University of Wollongong Asia.

Kabeer, N. (1999a). *The conditions and consequences of choice: Reflections on the measurement of women's empowerment.* UNSRID Discussion Paper No. 108. Geneva: UNSRID.

Kabeer, N. (1999b). Resources, agency, achievements: Reflections on the measurements of women's empowerment. *Development and Change, 30,* 435–464.

Kaur, A. (2007). International labour migration in Southeast Asia: Governance of migration and women domestic workers. *Intersections: Gender, History and Culture in the Asian Context.* Retrieved from http://intersections.anu.edu.au/issue15_contents.htm

Komnas, P., & Solidaritas, P. (2002). *Indonesian migrant workers: Systematic abuse at home and abroad.* Jakarta: Komnas Perempuan (Indonesian National Commission on Violence against Women) and Solidaritas Perempuan/CARAM Indonesia.

Komnas, P., & Solidaritas, P. (2003). *Indonesian migrant domestic workers: Their vulnerabilities and new initiatives for the protection of their rights (Indonesian country report to the UN special rapporteur on the human rights of migrants, 2003).* Jakarta: Komnas Perempuan (Indonesian National Commission on Violence against Women) and Solidaritas Perempuan/CARAM Indonesia.

Loveband, A. (2006). Positioning the product: Indonesian migrant women workers in Taiwan. In K. Hewison & K. Young (Eds.), *Transnational migration and work in Asia* (pp. 336–348). Abingdon: Routledge.

Pigay, N. (2005). *Migrasi tenaga kerja internasional: sejarah, fenomena, masalah dan solusinya.* Jakarta: Putaka Sinar Harapan.

Yamanaka, K., & Piper, N. (2005). *Feminized migration in East and Southeast Asia: Policies, actions and empowerment.* Retrieved July 30, 2006, from http://www.unrisd.org/unrisd/website/document.nsf/462fc27bd1fce00880256b4a0060d2af/06c975dec6217d4ec12571390029829a/$FILE/OP11%20web.pdf.

Yazid, S. (2013). *Indonesia's civil society in the age of democratization: NGO responses on the issue of labour migration.* Baden-Baden: Nomos.

Yazid, S., & Dewi, E. S. (2015). Women on the steering wheel: Identifying the potentials of women in improving the protection of Indonesian women migrant workers. *Journal of ASEAN Studies, 3*(2), 102–115.

Young, K. (2006). Globalization and the changing management of migrating service workers in the Asia-Pacific. In K. Hewison & K. Young (Eds.), *Transnational migration and work in Asia* (pp. 287–303). Abingdon: Routledge.

Sega as voice-work in the Indian Ocean region

Rosabelle Boswell

ABSTRACT
The island societies of the southwest Indian Ocean offer rich worlds
that reveal shared discourses regarding the natural environment,
politics and identity the region. This article draws on
anthropological research and in particular, recorded video for its
aesthetic analysis of voicework in Mauritius and Seychelles to
discuss the role of voicework in revealing cultural regionalization
and identity politics. It is proposed that the Sega (a musical
genre), its lyrics and performance, foreground shared identity and
responses to historical oppression in the region. The songs invoke
the islanders' resilience by referring to enduring elements in the
natural environment. African descendants in the islands use the
Sega and its performance, to locally (and naturally) embody
resistance to the historical elite. Following literatures on bodywork
in the social sciences, this article offers two concepts: voicework
and voicescape. Voicework is multisensory, trans-contextual,
impromptu and discursive expression in Sega music. The
voicescape refers to the often island-specific political and cultural
context generated by voicework. The article emphasizes the
embodied nature of voicework, anthropological research
experience and embodied social expression in the Indian Ocean
region (IOR).

*When you begin to see the possibilities of music, you desire to do something really good for
people, to help humanity free itself from its hang-ups.* John Coltrane

Introduction

The body has always been a socially complex terrain from which to pursue multiple ends
(Gill, Henwwood, and Maclean 2005; Gimlin, 2007; Mascia-Lewis, 2013; Tate, 2015). Bodies
are commoditized (van Wolputte, 2004) and enable diverse sexualities (Gill et al., 2005).
Bodies in action reveal moral purpose (Gimlin, 2007), fashion futures (Nyamnjoh & Fuh,
2014), curate lifestyles and the fleshliness of being human (Boswell, 2016). Embodiment,
a profoundly sensuous process (Bull & Back, 2003; Howes, 2010) is thought to produce holistic, situational and rich social experience. Inspired by the scholarship on bodywork,[1] this
article offers an analysis of voicework and voicescapes in two Indian Ocean islands:

Seychelles and Mauritius. By offering and examining voicework and voicescapes, the article hopes to nuance understanding of identity and music amongst the Creoles (people of African descent) living in Mauritius and Seychelles.

The discussion draws on anthropological research (1999–2016) ethnographic descriptions of live Sega performance and specifically recorded video for the aesthetic analysis of voicework. Generally, the discussion states that voicework in the two islands allows for non-violent responses to violent oppression. Voicework facilitates audibility in a still muting/aurally distorting environment. Situated at the bottom of the social and economic hierarchy, Creoles have been negatively stereotyped (Boswell, 2006). However, they still respond to those in power, countering both stately and scholarly noise (Hendy, 2013) via lyrics and music. The discussion reveals that voicework is a multisensory, bodily articulation of identity and experience. Voicework generates distinctive 'signatures' (i.e. voiceprints) to reveal social relations. It is discursive, impromptu, inventive and transcontextual (i.e. social, environmental and political) and it crafts a distinct social world that is parallel to, but separate from that which Creoles experience in the main. The world created is a distinctive voicescape, a vocal space indicating the regionalization of identity in the Indian Ocean region (IOR) and a *politically distinct place* from which Creoles can aerate particular concerns. In the live performances discussed in the article, voicework appears transient, evoking momentary sentiment and passing thought. Fleeting though these are, they always seem to speak to power. Voicework is not easily 'captured' or disciplined by those who publicly hold power.

The article concludes that voicework offers opportunities for a liberating emotional labor (Hoschild, 1979) and mutual intelligibility. In facial expression, vigor of dance move, pitch of vocal rendition and verbal twists, those engaged in song and dance use both body and voice to express emotions. I conclude with a reflection on my inclusion as an anthropologist in such emotional labors for the research process is always a politically implicating and mutually (but perhaps not equally) influencing process. I conclude that there may be amplified dominant voices in the voicescapes of the islands, however, these are disrupted by dissenting voices and critical ears, which help to reallocate meaning.

Theorizing voice

To theoretically analyze voice as something that offers insight into the regionalization and articulation of identity in the Indian Ocean, one needs to consider three overlapping contributions: the methodology and method of the researcher, the historically inscribed context in which the voices are embedded and third, contemporary social forces (i.e. globalization and creolization) and their influence on voices.

The disciplined voice

Considering the disciplinary context, early reflections on the discipline and the positioning of its practitioners (Asad, 1979; Clifford & Marcus, 1986; Mafeje, 1996) led to seminal discussions on the politics and poetics of voice in anthropology, especially the voice of the anthropologist in research (Boswell & Nyamnjoh, in Press). This history and theoretical reflection is relevant to the discussion because anthropologists have contributed substantively to sociocultural analyses of the Indian Ocean world and, in the past 40 years, anthropologists have been driven to acknowledge and engage with the dominance of their own voices in ethnographies. Today, many offer self-reflexive and politically conscious scholarship. But first, it was mostly liberal feminists who interrogated the role of voice in intelligibility and representation (Abu-Lughod, 1991; Hastrup, 1995; Moore, 1994; Spivak, 1988). In this context, the voices of black women anthropologists remained largely absent because few attained positions of seniority or influence within the academy. As a black anthropologist desiring to achieve a measure of influence, I also sought to 'hear' northern voices and to echo these in prescriptive (i.e. publication) channels.

All anthropologists however, now re-oriented, are expected to *lift silences* and *render audible* historical practice (Depelchin, 2005). All are expected to authentically *give voice* to their research participants. All are required to scrutinize their own authorial voice, as though everyone has always been able to make themselves heard. Contemporary African anthropologists originating from diverse social worlds experience scholarly challenges. Can they reveal the richness of their own voices, if they have been trained to articulate a 'masterly' Euro-American voice? Can they produce a new grounded scholarship, if most of the theoretical contribution emanates from the global north and the latter is perceived as the source of reputable output? In this article, I show that one needs a critical ear to avoid missing alternative, radically creative and resilient knowledge forms.

Recent theorizations of voice emphasize the importance of retaining one's voice. These suggest that once distorted, it is difficult to fully recover an authentic voice, for voices emerge in multi-vocal and yet politically inscribing worlds (Weidman, 2014). In that kind of context, it takes great effort to still hear oneself, let alone alternative voices. In the IOR, a place of multiple globalizations, African descendants' voices are also continuously positioned. Long-term contact and exchange in the region and external social forces, such as environmental change and tourism displace their voicings and what is left, are inferiorly represented and often distorted. Analyzing the Sega as voicework, I hope to shift attention from form and analysis to show that voicework is multisensory and multidimensional. This involves cognitive and political work, since there are many voices making their way into the voicescapes of the Seychelles and Mauritius. These overlap and are contested. Noisy leaders impose their own voicings, scholars add their pitch and local residents want to be heard too. In the conclusion and throughout the discussion, I hint at the necessity and presence of the critical ear. An ear that listens to hear rather than one seeking merely to analyze.

Noisy leaders

Noisy leaders produce their own cacophonous and discursive voicescape. In the post-colonial nations of Seychelles and Mauritius, leaders regularly and vocally bring the past into the present contributing to dominant voicework. Historically advantaged elites add to this, strategically, audibly and visibly endorsing nostalgic voicings of the past (Salverda, 2015). Needing the symbolic power to actualize political ambitions, noisy leaders rely on simplified representations of culture to achieve political ends. UNESCO has made their task easier, globally amplifying cultural practices and sites by inscribing them on a universally honored World Heritage List (WHL). The inscribed UNESCO World Heritage Sites in both Seychelles and Mauritius (briefly noted further on) generate narratives of cohesive nationhood and bounded identity. Thus in Mauritius, World Heritage celebrates nostalgic, ethnic accounts of the past and in Seychelles it emphasizes pristine nature and its conservation. Reasonable accounts of the past and of appropriately safeguarded natural environments advance economically profitable and politically expedient narratives of nationhood. The ultimate aim is to realize tourist desire, for visitors need culture to be intelligible and locals to be acquiescent. No-one wants to be deprived of the fantasy of a racially 'ordered' and yet exotic destination.

Scholars and novelists are nuancing noisy voicework. Alluding to inhabitants as members of a cultural oikumene or 'region,' Gurnah, Ghosh, Naipaul and Collen refer to the flows, eddies and waves of contact and exchange in the IOR (Gurnah, 2001; Ghosh, 2011; Collen, 1995; Naipaul, 1972). They also write about intercultural conversations, linguistic creolization and shared feelings of displacement. Historians of the region concur, indicating historical and cultural interconnectedness (Allen, 2001; Campbell, 1988; Randrianja and Ellis, 2009; Shell, 1994; Sheriff, 1987; Teelock, 1998; Ward & Worden, 1998). Alpers (2000) even calls the region Indian Ocean Africa, emphasizing the islanders' historical connections with the continent and the role of Africa in shaping island societies and cultures.

The folklorist Haring (2002, 2004) delves more deeply into voicings in the islands, examining linguistic and verbal expression. Ethnographies add yet another layer. Compelling ethnographies (Graeber, 2007; Jeffrey, 2007; Ramamonjisoa, 2001; Salverda, 2015; Sharp, 1995, 2001) seem to advance northerly analyses, in which the voices of islanders emerge as evidence to support (sometimes) 'bodiless' accounts where there are profoundly embodied realities. In the following, I suggest that all voices are profoundly mediated and that in the 'field,' one cannot deny the intersubjective process of the research. For me, voicework is both concept and journey. A means to reground my voice in a multisensory and embodied world. This article then, hopes to bring a critical fragment to the global discussion on mutuality and the politics of the research process, that is, social research in the region might consider bodily and facial expressions not only as analyzable things but also as potential frameworks for understanding the IOR. Haring (2002, 2004) has already said that voicings in the IOR contain innuendo, double-entendres, metaphors, here I add that they audibly and bodily articulate a distinct 'space,' producing a sort of *third space* (Bhabha, 1994) or, as I have called it here, a voicescape.

Voices in and voicing the Indian Ocean world

The Jazz musician, John Coltrane thought that music is key to liberation or at the very least, enabled humanity to get rid of its 'hang-ups.' John Cage, a composer, deepened this thought. Producing a blank score, which he entitled 4' 33, Cage argued that there is 'no such thing as silence,' for even when one remains silent, there are other sounds which one can still hear.[2] Given what has been said about voicework possibly producing a third space for identity and response to historical oppression in the region, I next flesh out how voicework might reveal a unique *voicescape* and whether this disrupts the noise made by leaders and scholars publicly shaping voice in the IOR. As already stated, the discussion interrogates these issues by focusing on the Sega, especially in Mauritius and Seychelles.

A few people have written in broad terms about the Sega. However, the emphasis has been on the technical form of song and dance genre, as well as the instruments used.

Drawing on fieldwork in Mauritius and Seychelles, as well as video materials, the next part of the discussion focuses on the context of the islands as well as context created by the musicians. I argue that the Sega is diverse, produces a regional voicescape but also specific voiceprints. These in turn, reveal the stoicism, resilience, playfulness and eloquence of Creoles in the islands. I also suggest that the Sega creates a 'hived' off world, that reveals Alpers' 'Indian Ocean Africa.' To get to the song and dance, an introduction to the islands is necessary. This briefly prefaces the following part of the discussion.

Contexts and varieties: Sega, song and dance

Many global citizens now know that Mauritius is an island situated in the IOR. In the twenty-first century, it is associated with internationally renowned recreational tourism, peaceful multiculturalism, economic growth and progressive politics. It has a population of 1.3 million, many of whom are multilingual and multicultural. However, a significant population of African descended people, locally defined as Creoles are part of the island society. Creoles also populate nearby islands such as Reunion and Rodrigues, they dominate the ethnic grouping in Seychelles, an archipelago of some 90 coral islands to the north of Mauritius. The Creoles of Mauritius and Seychelles speak a French-based language that includes Swahili, Bhojpuri, Hindi and English. In each island, the language, referred to as *Kreol*, varies. It varies across villages, generations, subcultures and class, but that is a complex matter to be discussed elsewhere.

Historians (Allen, 2001; Teelock, 1998) confirm that Mauritius was originally *Terra Nullius* and that the population settled there and in nearby island territories, over a period of 180 years. Specifically, Mauritius was first settled in the seventeenth century by the Dutch, then the French (1715) and subsequently the English in 1810. 'Settlement' however, euphemistically describes the actual circumstances of human arrival to the island. In brief, the colonial powers enslaved Africans and forcibly relocated them to Mauritius, keeping many generations of Africans in bondage until abolition in 1835. Thereafter, they 'replaced' the slaves with Indian indentured laborers. The slaves, taken from Madagascar and the east/southern coast of Africa, came either from present day Mozambique or further inland, since Mauritius still retains place names and surnames reminiscent of ethnicities beyond southern Africa. Some 60,000 people were forced into slavery.

The Seychelles did not escape this dreadful history. Under French rule from about 1788, slaves were transported to the archipelago as the property of slave owners with land concessions there. In Mauritius, slaves worked on sugar plantations and in the Seychelles they worked on coconut plantations. It is impossible (here) to fully articulate the specific histories of both islands, except to add that from 1861 the Seychelles received various consignments of slaves whom the British had freed from Arab dhows. The consignments were promptly redirected to the British Seychelles colony. The freed slaves renewed the island's African descendants' knowledge of east Africa, its main languages and cultural ethos.

The plantation narratives of both islands find expression in the voicework of Creoles in both the recent past and today. As noted further on, the islanders sing about the dreariness of plantation work, the need for resilience, desire for vengeance and ongoing oppression. Colonialism, which swiftly followed after the abolition of slavery, further inspired lyrics and the diversification of the Sega. Influenced by the aesthetic and performative imperative of colonialism, the African descendants produced new dances and incorporated into their performance of the Sega, instruments emanating from England, Scotland and France. These performances often took place beyond the purview of those in control. Mauritians produced the Sega tipik (traditional Sega) a genre that was often also *engage*, that is, politically salient. From the 1960s, they produced other songs and home-based dance (*Sega Salon*) that was reflective of the modernizing society. In the Seychelles, there was the *Sega tipik* and the *Moutia* (a slow Sega) and *Contre-danse*. *Contre-danse* sounds distinctly like a Scottish jig and dancers are expected to move in a square 'formation.' In Rodrigues island, a dependency of Mauritius, there is the *Polkarisse*, an iteration of the *Contre-danse*. Derived from Polka, *Polkarisse* was modified by the Rodrigues islanders who came into contact with Scottish missionaries. In Reunion there is the *Maloya* (Boswell, 2006). All of these are indicative of the regionalization and diversity of the Sega.

From the late 1800s to the present day, individual Sega singers and groups emerged. There has also been significant change in the Sega. The adaptation of Sega into *Seggae* (a blend of reggae and Sega) for instance, now articulates new economic priorities and political imperatives. *Seggae* created by the Creole singer Kaya and Rasnatty Baby in the 1990s Mauritius gives voice to a now regionally expressed 'black pain' (Boswell, 2006). This pain is 'voiced' across the islands.

Sega performance in the past, as it is now, involves a soloist and possible 'backing' singers. There are instruments that are not (as I explain further on) entirely local. The *ravanne*, *maravanne*, triangle (and in modern times, guitars) form part of the instruments accompanying the Sega.

The singers of Sega also vary and most enjoy considerable reputation. In recent times, the Sega has transformed. It is now sung by people who are not 'visibly' of African descent. Sega is performed in hotels and it is rendered 'authentic' by staged performances on beaches. In the past 15–20 years, many Sega singers have traveled to Europe to perform in Europe and Australia.[3] Online viewings of these concerts suggest that members of the audience are predominantly Mauritian or from the islands. The concerts seem to facilitate nostalgia and memory-making, as well as nationalist solidarity in a globalized space. Sega however is equally influenced by other solidarities. It is gendered and classed. The songs tell of women's experiences of emotional and sexual relationships and they speak to class distinctions. The varieties of Sega, its gendered aspects, as well as its localization create an impression that Sega (as voice) is so diverse that it does not have anything in common.

Transgressions, oppositions and play

In the following part of the discussion, I offer anthropological fieldwork data that explain the embeddedness of Sega, its commonalities, varied purposes and experience of it in different locales. This is so that one can see that Sega does have common objectives and that voicework is indeed multisensory, impromptu, discursive and trans-contextual.

The relevance of context

During anthropological fieldwork in Mauritius in 1999, I met an old Creole man in Le Morne village on the west coast of Mauritius. Locally known as *Ti* Roland, he explained that he was the last *bobre* (zither) player in Mauritius. But before telling me about the village and his place in it, he told me that a truly pleasurable life was one in which you could be free to play the music that made your heart sing. With great patience, he explained exactly how Sega evolved in the region around Le Morne Brabant (Boswell, 2006). His story emphasized the embeddedness of Sega in the lives of Creoles. He recalled seeing villagers along the west coast and in the hills of the Black River Gorges, coming to Le Morne village every weekend to dance, play music, sing and drink. Music and dance was a collective activity that enabled Creoles to release the stress and burden of hard labor experienced on the island's sugar plantations. At that time (the 1930s) Creoles living on the west coast were for the most part, either employed on the same plantations from which their enslaved ancestors had been liberated, or they had opted for a less circumscribed life as subsistence fishermen. *Ti* Roland went on, Fishermen, he said, woke early in the morning to set their fish traps or set out to the reef. The journey was one which required great care. It involved 'reading' the sky the day before, looking closely at the sea and waves in the morning, memorizing the seascape so as to know where to 'harvest.' Each journey was carefully timed; fishermen observed the sea/sky and did not overestimate their skill. Not all who ventured out to sea were men. Women, he explained, harvested seafood in the tidal zone, had boats of their own and set out in groups. *Ti* Roland's stories of Le Morne confirm that context is relevant to understanding the multidimensionality of the Sega and the multisensory nature not only of voicework but also (and more broadly) social existence.

In the Seychelles, I found a similar trans-contextual voicework. In the Sega of the Seychellois, there is regular reference to steep hills, heavily wooded forests, winding roads, fishing and the ever present breadfruit. The monsoon season encourages the island's large breadfruit trees to produce a bounty of fruit throughout the year. Observing the natural environment in the main island of Mahé, I noticed (in 2005) the reflection of the green hills and forests in the island's crystal waters. Daily, dark green leaves would drip heavily from passing rain showers, nourishing the soil beneath.

Running to shelter from a sudden cloud burst in the hilly village of Takamaka, one morning, I found myself in an empty church, peering through a window. Through it I saw villagers slipping and sliding down the hill to the road, whilst others stoically climbed upwards, facing the driving rain. Some were carrying baskets laden with breadfruit whilst others were holding the vegetable by the stem. The people with breadfruit image stayed in mind, for a few days earlier, a sculptor in a village not much further away explained that after the Seychelles became a socialist regime in 1979, everyone was 'reduced to breadfruit.' There were no longer any class distinctions and everyone was forced to eat the same thing. In addition, regular shortages of basic commodities meant that people had little access to imported goods and had to rely on the natural environment. Breadfruit, hardship, stoicism are recurrent themes in the Sega of the Seychellois.

Context then, diverse and differently situated is immensely important to understanding articulations of voice. Nature seems ever present in Indian Ocean voicework. It is the rainy weather, the hills, the unpredictable and yet liberating sea, the relentlessness of plantation work and the spices of the islands that makes its way into the particular voicescape in the Indian Ocean islands.

The father of traditional Sega in Mauritius, ironically called *Ti* frère[4] (little brother), born in the late 1880s, was adept at conveying a multiply layered context in his Segas. *Ti* frère led the development of the *Sega tipik*. Others following him, such as Serge Lebrasse, Roger Clency, Jean Claude Gaspard, Marie Josée Clency and more recently Linzy Bacbotte, continue the work of rearticulating socio-political and environmental context. *Ti frère* tells about his environment (the village, his house and economic circumstances). He advances the Sega as a contribution to a transgressive/oppositional voicescape. His Segas speak for alternative norms, values and practices. A discussion of his songs and the songs of other *Segatiers* (Sega singers) is offered further on. In the next section, I describe several live performances of the Sega, hoping to confirm the embodied nature of the dance, as well as its multisensory and interactive aspects.

Sega is sung in the community, on the beaches, in homes. There is homemade rum, culturally specific snacks, references to work on plantations and struggles with the sea. Using instruments that appear elsewhere in the musical genres of the Indian Ocean world, Sega does not sugar coat the realities of poverty and struggle. Sega is sung by men and women, it includes sexual innuendo, overtly sexualized (read: improper) conduct and it indicates verbal articulacy – the latter having never been associated with slave descendants. Thus, Sega (and its associated social context and behaviors) allows African descendants to hive off a meaningful space, where they can *sing back* to the white, oppressive ideals of 'high' culture, propriety and chasteness.

The transgressive nature of the songs (and the social contexts generated for the dances) is evident in that Africans in Mauritius and Seychelles did not do much to dispel the negative discourse of the Sega as a dance of 'low' culture, lasciviousness and immorality. The African descendants continued to imbibe vast quantities of alcohol at the dances, danced by the firelight on the beach and persisted in their use of drums and goat skin *ravannes*. Dances devolved into fights, especially fights in defense of honor. In recent years, the transgressive elements of the Sega have been diluted. Social mores have relaxed and societies in the islands have become more sexually permissive. The boom in recreational tourism (sun, sea and sex) is making the 'transgressions' that are less transgressive. I next offer three ethnographic descriptions of Sega in Mauritius, to offer a feel of the embodied and multisensory nature of the genre.

Performance
In the village. In August 1999, during fieldwork in a village on the east coast of the island, I witnessed the profoundly interactive and multisensory nature of Sega. It was a day on which the country was celebrating the International Day for the Celebration of Creole Languages and Cultures (*Journée Internationale de la langue et de la culture Creoles*) and emerging Creole politicians had begun to establish linkages with South African politicians. Under the leadership of a former South African president, Thabo Mbeki and his philosophy of African Renaissance, the latter seemed keen to advance connections with the African diaspora. It was also on that same year a Nelson Mandela Centre for African Culture was inaugurated. The day in the village was delightfully dry for August in the southern hemisphere, the inhabitants were clearly excited. I had taken a bus from a nearby village to attend and I, along with the others waited quite some time for the politicians to appear. The festivities, we were told, could not start until they had arrived. Girl children, aged between 5 and 12 were dressed in brightly colored cropped floral tops and long, wide skirts. Carefully coiffed and made up, they waited anxiously for the call to dance. Boys, also young in age (the youngest appeared to be four years old), waited close by.

Three men sat in one corner to the yard where the performance was to take place. A few chickens crossed the floor, pecking at imaginary grains on the hardened ground. Unnoticed, they eventually edged themselves into the background away from the awaiting audience. The latter consisted mostly of adult women and men, who leaned against walls or sat on a tree stumps. Some of the women, their hair in curlers, had not 'dressed' for the occasion. I noticed they kept looking back towards their houses, every now and then barking an instruction to a child or family member to go and turn the heat down on lunch. An irresistible aroma of *rougaille* (red piquant sauce) filled the air, doubtless, I hungrily imagined, to cover an equally fresh and succulent fried tail of red mullet. Hungry and hot in the afternoon sun, the audience waited for the politicians to arrive. Finally, and after about two hours, they appeared, accompanied by what appeared to be the French Ambassador to Mauritius, the South African High Commissioner and his entourage. Dressed in 'African' print and tie-dye shirts, they were given chairs to sit on. Soon enough though, the three men in the corner of the yard began to beat their *ravannes*. These released deep drum-like sounds that resonated through the bodies of those standing near enough to them. Holding the *ravannes* on their knees, gripping one side to hold it steady, they used their remaining hands, letting these rise and fall on the taut and fired goat skin to produce multiply layered beats. The sound seemed to pull up and out of my chest a heaviness that had long resided there. I could feel it coming up from my chest and into my throat. My eyes welled up with tears that I had not expected, which in turn, rolled down my face forcing me to wipe them away quickly lest anyone I hoped to interview later on, saw. I focused on the men with the *ravannes*, rivulets of sweat slid down the sides of their faces, as if issued by their dreadlocks. Their thin arms and gnarled hands prominent with raised veins flexed and released as they relentlessly beat the *ravannes*. To their left, were boys, probably about four of them and each held a small *ravanne, triangle, capsil* or small *djembe* drum. Each child intently and rhythmically engaged his instrument, watching the three men to keep up with the beat. The girls moved onto the hardened soil of the yard. Barefoot, they moved in unison, their small hips rising and falling with the beat. One hand the hip and another to hold up the tip of the long skirt. It is not long before some of the villagers abandon their much coveted tree stumps to join the dance. Circling one another, couples take on gender-specific moves. The men stretch out their arms, one leg back the other forward, they gyrate their hips, at once symbolically protecting 'their' woman whilst also publicly demonstrating sexual potential. The women respond in kind, suggestively moving their hips and buttocks, looking back (and this time, not to their kitchen) but to 'their' man, to give him the attention he deserves. The deep rolling beat of the *ravannes*, the high pitch ring of the *triangle*, the whoops and laughter of the villagers mingle in the now blazing heat of the afternoon sun. Unable to resist, the African Commissioner joins the dance. In the corner of my eye, I catch a glimpse of an old woman's face. Seated under a tree, she looks on, her eyes smiling at the spectacle. I wonder if she is remembering a youthful moment experienced or, whether she is happy for having witnessed the reunion of Africans distanced by history.

On the beach. Sega on the beach and at night may be different to that observed in the daytime. In 2000, again on the east coast of the island, my husband and I went for an evening walk on a moonlit beach. We were surprised by darting, seemingly disembodied lights in the distance. Approaching these, I soon realized that there were crab hunters, using torches to light up the holes newly drilled by sea crabs that came to the shore at night. Passing the crab hunters, we heard a distant rumbling. It was the sound of *ravannes* that naturally grew louder as we approached. We soon came upon a corner of the beach where a few people had gathered. Once more, two men were seated on stones, their dreadlocks hanging loose down their backs. On their knees were the *ravannes*. A third *ravanne* was being lightly warmed over a fire, to make the goat skin tauter, so that when hit, its pitch would be perfect. There were two women dancers. Both wore ordinary skirts and their tops were knotted and tucked up into their brassieres. They began to dance, long before the drumming began or a song escaped the lips of the *Segatier*. Languidly undulating their hips, their faces illuminated by the orange fire emanating from the pit dug into the sand. They seemed to move to an as yet unheard Sega, a memory of a song. They did not dance in unison. Rather, each produced her own style and rhythm, circling the fire, gesticulating elegant fingers in the air, faces solemn, almost as if they were contemplating the seriousness of the dance. The *Segatier*, an old Creole woman broke into song. It was about the ancestors, their legacies, their pain and fact of the blood of slavery still running through the singer's veins. The people watching did not dance. They watched, arms folded, equally solemn and seemingly equally contemplative. Halfway through the song, the women slowly went down on to their knees. In unison they bent backwards, still undulating their hips. Then, with the tips of their fingers, they touched the sand and let their hair tumble onto it. The *Segatier* stopped singing and the *ravanne* players amplified the beat. The women curled their bodies upwards, rising a notch at a time from the sand. First their fingers from the sand, then their hair, then the chest followed by the still moving hips and finally rising from the ground, they stand up and circled the fire again.

In a center. In July 2015, I revisited Le Morne village to interview some of the inhabitants and to find out if their lives had changed for the better after the inscription of Le Morne Brabant on the WHL in 2008. I was also curious to see if there had been any further development insofar as the place of Sega in Mauritius is concerned, since the dance had also been given World Heritage status in 2014. I came across a group of brightly dressed women followed by their *Segatier*, they had been hired to dance at the event organized by the Le Morne Heritage Trust Fund (LMTF). The latter had been set up after the site's inscription in 2008, to manage the representation of heritage in the village and the development of heritage resources for tourism purposes. A full discussion on the politics and organization of LMTF is not possible here, however, it was clear that in 2015, Sega was also being performed in other voicescapes.

I arrived at the LMTF offices late in the morning. I was one of a few visitors to the offices and the stalls which they set up on that day. Unlike the experience in the village in 1999 and on the beach in 2000, the dancing on the side of the road seemed futile, lonely and inauthentic. In brief, there seemed to be several multisensory aspects missing. There was no fire, no village aesthetic, there was no moonlight to create a magical atmosphere nor was there the aroma of local food to foster a sense of being in a particular place. The dancers looked strained. They danced the same steps, gyrated their hips in the same manner to the thin ringing of a *triangle*, lost in the sound of cars driving by. An amplifier and CD Player was placed on a table next to the dancers to accompany the sound of the musical instruments. Played at loud volume to attract passers-by, the music and the dance failed to elicit a feeling of voicescape – that unique space for the articulation of thoughts and feelings not usually expressed in public.

Most Sega, as I have already suggested, seems to facilitate 'escape' or *defoulement* from the overbearing reality of oppression. Sega also seems to encourage facing or playful engagement with pain. At certain moments, the songs can expressively articulate victim-hood (there is the gravelly tone of voice, use of traditional instruments and solemn, worn faces), not long after, the opposite can happen, singers make fun of the downfall of a fellow villager, his troubles and his lack of intelligence. Clothing and the movement of dancers also suggests an ambivalence. In the village in 1999 and on the beach in 2000, I caught glimpses of the embodied and multisensory nature of Sega. In 2015 however, when I visited Le Morne, I did not see this. Instead, I witnessed an almost soulless perform-ance of identity, a desperate bid to retain the dynamism of culture in the face of increasing fixity and the circumscribing of identity (Figure 1).

The limitation of Sega's multisensory nature is perhaps apparent in the manipulation of the tactile dress worn by dancers. Dancers of the Sega *tipik* are now often seen wearing the kind of clothing usually worn by slave descendants who worked on the sugar plantations in the Caribbean. In one image of Sega dancers (on the UNESCO site) there seems to be an attempt to render Sega respectable. There is no flesh shown and all the performers are wearing white clothing (Figure 2).

Secondly and as previously described, the Sega is physically demanding, requiring deep awareness of one's physical limits and flexibility. As described, about halfway through the

Figure 1. Sega, Le Morne. 2015. Photo courtesy Rosabelle Boswell (authors own).

song, there is an interregnum, a pause, filled only by drumbeats, the sound of *ravannes* and triangle. The dancers lower themselves to the ground and on their knees. If there is a couple, their bodies circle one another. Great flexibility and strength is required of both. Both must gradually (and in beat) lower themselves to the floor. The woman must bend her back, so that her head will touch the ground. The man must lean forwards over her, not touching her but still move his body to continue the dance. Third, and as also already described, context, movement, facial expression and words seamlessly interweave to produce a holistic and embodied experience of the genre. Thus, voice is not merely the vocal or the audible, it forms part of the body politic (Figure 3).

Inexperienced dancers, unengaged dancers and arrhythmic dancers tend to develop a great deal of pain and stiffness in the leg which they favor. Sega is not just about the mechanics of moving the right body part at the right time and in sync with one's partner, it offers a place and metaphor with which to express the importance of timeliness and the need for balanced participation in a socially inscribed context. Whilst singers sing, dancers must wait their turn to demonstrate their prowess. They need to dance considering the needs and intention of others on the floor. A faux pas does not necessarily bring embarrassment but it can upset the synchronicity of movement and the joy derived from fluid, considerate and rhythmic movement.

Wordplay

A closer look at the lyrics of Sega music offers further insight into its multidimensionality and the ways in which it creates both voicescapes and voiceprints. In Mauritian Sega we see transgressive thoughts and values that emerge in wordplay. In Seychellois lyrics we see

Figure 2. An image of Sega. http://www.unesco.org/culture/ich/en/RL/traditional-mauritian-sega-01003. Accessed 26 September 2016.

Figure 3. Sega Dancer's head touches the ground. Source: http://www.maurice-info.mu/decisions-du-conseil-ministres-du-14-novembre-2014.html. Accessed 26 September 2016.

stoicism and lamentations. In both island societies, the lyrics mention the natural environment, historical events, class and gender relations, taste, aesthetics and emotions. In both, the dancing is symbolically rich.

In Mauritius, *Ti* frère's *Amina*, transgressions are nuanced via euphemized speech. The woman in the story, a woman of Indian descent, is encouraged to stay the night on the understanding that *Ti* frère will 'accompany' her home in the morning. The singer it seems employs various innuendoes. First, it is a chaste Indian woman whom a Creole man is enticing. Second, in Mauritius, the word 'accompany' holds particular meaning. It hints at the gentlemanly act of chaperoning, which in this case, a dubious Creole man is trying to pull off. Third, a lady chaperoned is one who is not to be taken advantage of. The singer goes on to entreat her by saying '*rentre dans mo lakaz, vine guette endans mo l'armoire*' (come into my house and look inside my cupboard), pretending that he has only honorable intentions in asking her to join him for the night.

But there is more to the Sega of *Ti* frère than his words and intended meanings. His voice, like Satchmo's brown-bread gravelly tone, the instruments of the ensemble: triangle, *ravanne*, *capsil* (metal bottle caps) and spoons tied together, produce an externally unmediated sound that can only be replicated in the outdoors. If one listens carefully, there are other voices. Pausing between his encouragements, women singers fill the gap with a repetitive response, articulating the popular form of call-and-response found in musical performance in east Africa.

Transgression and its consequences are also emphasized in the Sega 'Bal ran Zarico'[5] the Party of the Return of the Bean. Popular in both Mauritius and Seychelles, the aim of this party is to place a bean in a cake and whoever obtains the slice that contains the bean has to host the next party. In this song, the Mauritian singer, Roger Clency (who composed this song in the 1970s, a time when Mauritians were working hard to produce a modern nation), speaks of Titire, a pompous man and his wife, who host such a party. Showing off their newfound class status, evident in the choice of snacks offered to their guests, Titire and his wife set out to dance the Tango, not the Sega. Titire is unable to attain the status to which he aspires. He serves typically *Ti Kreol* (lower class Creole) snacks, such as roast tenrec drumsticks, he drinks too much and invites a portly woman (not his wife) to dance. Instead of daintily holding her waist, he accidentally grabs her behind. Defending her honor, the woman's husband takes Titire to task, beating him up in front of guests. The next day, bruised and rather the worse for wear, Titire resolves to never host a Bean Return Party again.

This particular song also shows the extensive preparation for Sega parties and performances. The preparation itself helps to constitute community. Since Sega was perceived by whites as a sexualized dance of slave descendants, the latter, along with their Indian neighbors attempted to improve the Sega by keeping it to the *salon* (lounge), itself a marker of middle-class status. Whites, whether in Mauritius or the Seychelles only 'invited' blacks into their social environment as domestic workers and laborers. In both islands, Sega was publicly associated with notoriety, poor taste, ineloquence and blackness. The situation was exacerbated by the fact that *Sega tipik* singers often sing of the 'the blood of slaves rising' within them ('*disan esclave pé monter dans mo lekor*'), referring to their desire for restitution, the pain of past dispossession and acknowledgement of slavery itself. Many Sega songs in both Seychelles and Mauritius contain references to blackness. There is '*mo noir*' (my black), '*grand noir*' (show off), '*ti noir*' (vagabond) and '*le temps margoze*' (time of bitterness).

Preparations for the parties also add a distinct flavor to the Sega and its social world. 'Brewers' of local rum would begin concocting the brew a few days ahead of the party. In the Seychelles, it was learned that the brewing of alcohol, specifically *baca* and many different kinds of *rhum arrangée* (fruity, homemade rum) was a skill passed on from one generation to the next. Homemade alcohol accompanied each Sega performance but brewing alcohol was illegal and the task had to be done in secret. If discovered, the brewers would bribe the policemen with a *grogue* (a drink) or two.

Another feature (also mentioned in the song of Titire) is food. *Gajack* (snacks) formed an integral part of the Sega party. Grilled *cochon marron* (wild boar), *tangues* or *ti vitesses* (tenrecs) made it to the snack tables. Known informally as *gajack*, such snacks (indicative of both class and ethnicity) were imperative for proper appreciation and energetic participation in the Sega. The snacks are also meaningful in other senses, since at least in the 1960s and 1970s, both the tenrec and wild boar, as well as most of what is obtainable from the sea and rivers was obtained by men, who formed special hunting and fishing groups to get these meats. In 2016, a research participant, who is an avid computer programmer, occasional fisherman and tenrec hunter, said that very few people (men) were hunting, since the culling and selling of tenrecs was now a 'business.' He hastened to add that the tenrecs were no longer tasty (*tangues népli éna gout*). At Sega dances, the presence of particular food and drink symbolizes and accounts for empowered masculinity.

The cooked tenrec (implying that hunting has happened), masculine brewing of alcohol both emphasize an alternatively grounded identity for men oppressed in a racialized society.

Stoicism and lamentation

Sega songs across the islands of Mauritius and Seychelles reveal alternative, parallel expressions of identity. In the following, it is also added that the Sega reveals the stoicism and resilience of Creoles. These counter the political and scholarly narrative of them as victims, oppressed by slavery and colonialism. In his song, *Moi mo ène ti Creole*[6] (I am just a little Creole), the singer, Serge Lebrasse tells of how a teacher beats a little Creole boy for speaking 'his version' of Creole. This would seem to convince us that yes, Creoles are victims. Impersonating the child however, he goes on to say that since both his mother and father are Creole, he cannot be anything else, for 'out of a chicken egg, one cannot hatch a duckling.' No matter, Lebrasse says, Creoles, especially *'ti'* Creoles should remain authentic, for 'we know our true value.'

In their songs, the Seychellois regularly make references to their natural environment and the resources in it. Breadfruit appears in song, riddles and references to politics. In the song Kololo by the group Still Waters, the singers encourage Kololo, a grave digger by telling him, *'pas bizin pleurer, Kololo, pas bizin, pas bizin pleurer, l'année prochain ou a gagne tout c'est ki ou a content'* (don't cry, Kololo, don't cry, next year you'll get everything your heart desires). They carry on,

> we see you climbing that hill every day, at dusk, you climb back down, every day going down with your spade, every night going back up with just two breadfruits. Don't worry Kololo, don't worry, next year you'll get everything you want.

They even tell him how to manage this monotonous hardship, *'dousman, dousman mignon, dousman dousman couma l'habitude'* (slowly, slowly my dear, slowly slowly as you usually do').

In the Seychellois Joseph Louise's song[7] also about the *Ti* Creoles (*Ti Kreol Leo*), the singer impersonates a Creole man and sings about him coming down from the hills to work on the plantation. He says that he is a Creole *le haut* – from above, on the hills and he will never let his honor fall in the sea (be besmirched), he works on the plantation, in the hot sun without a shirt (without protection) but still works hard, with dignity. The Sega singer, Jacob Marie, more popularly known as Tonpa, who, like *Ti* Roland (from Mauritius) played the *bobre* (pronounced as *bomn* in Seychelles) also sang of dignity, honesty and authenticity. In a YouTube documentary on Tonpa, the popular (and also Seychellois singer) Jean-marc Volcy says that the songs of Tonpa has made him into a cultural singer.[8] Another interviewee says that Tonpa's Sega offers a caricature of Seychellois society and the place of Creoles in it. The songs speak of strategy (*démarche*), ways in which to 'tromper la vie' (deal with life/trick fate). Volcy specifically says that singers like Tonpa had the ability to almost make members of the audience believe that the song is about their lives. When confronted on a 'bad' message, he would simply say that this is but a *zistwar* (a story not to be taken seriously).

Increasing numbers of women in both islands are also singing Sega. Their words open up the 'world' of women in the islands, revealing symbols of femininity and critical engagement with such symbols. It is women singers, such as Marie Josée Clency and more recently, Linzy Bacbotte and Nancy Derougere who articulate these issues. Their songs are full of vivid imagery. Clency began to sing in the 1970s. Her songs reflect increasing feminism in Mauritius after its independence from colonial rule. In her song, 'Mother I want to get married,' the singer adopts the voice of a young woman who rejects the advice of her sage mother. Marrying a *galand* (a dandy), she soon finds herself burdened, '*astère difé lor moi, dourri di l'eau mo pe tomber dormi*' (today I'm under fire, 'eating' rice water, I fall asleep), because the young man is '*dominère*' (abusive). Bacbotte on the other hand, who became famous after the national race riots of 1999, articulates a post-colonial, pro-negritude ethos in her songs. Together with her husband, Bruno Raya, who performs the identity of 'authentic' Creole manhood by respecting his African roots in public; Bacbotte sings of ideal love, devoid of desires for material advancement. Derougère is less convinced. She does not seem to romanticize romance or Creole manhood. In a song called *Laké Poilon* [9](the Frying Pan's Tail), she speaks to the rising power of women in Mauritius and its effects on the employment and education of men. She says 'it is I who know the heat of the frying pan, I am both man and woman in this house, everyday it's give and give, there will be a time when I can give no more,' adding that it is 'the one who holds the hot "tail" of the frying pan that knows the heat.' When her husband wants something it is always 'yes,' whilst her words are like '*di l'eau lor feuille bredes songes*' (water off a [hydrophobic] taro leaf).

Derougère and Bacbotte are millennial singers in the history of the Sega. Long before they arrived on the scene, Creole women like Clency were singing about the effects of World War II on Mauritius. In a famous Sega entitled '*Repran mo mari Anglais*'[10] (Take my husband back Englishman), the singer exhorts the English to take her husband back after World War II, for he has changed too much for her to endure him.[11] Referring to the effects of war, Clency says that her husband is no longer the same, he refuses to speak *Kreol*, choosing rather to articulate himself in a bastardized version of English. He has also forgotten that breakfast in Mauritius does not consist of bacon and eggs. It is only when walking along the beach one day and a crab pinches his foot, that he curses and screams '*ayo Crabe bez mo le doight*' (oh damn, the bloody crab bit me!). The singer, taking on the persona of a 'wife' goes on to say that the English must take her husband back, '*zotte a faire saussisson are li*' (you can make sausages with him), stereotyping the English as a sausage-eating lot.

The songs of the Seychellois and Mauritians produce mutually intelligible worlds for the inhabitants. The voicings offer a profound, funny and intelligent take on a world in which there was and still is a great deal of violence. Memory, dance and eloquence, it seems, are the things which African descendants retained and developed after slavery. Today, these facilitate a particular social world, a voicescape of sorts in the region.[12] As the novelists already mentioned suggest, the islanders are connected by a history of slavery and trans-oceanic travel. It is not only rhythm and metaphors crossing the waters but also parts of languages, instruments and philosophies. The last point is, I think, quite important. It suggests that in the midst of slavery and colonization there was significant creativity and resilience, especially through song. Songs enable a sharing of experience, empathetic advice, cries for help and appeals to retain dignity despite the fact that it is being stripped from one's person.

Conclusion: the politics of voicework

In 2014 Sega was inscribed on UNESCO's WHL. This is a significant step forward for the genre, as there is now global recognition for it as a universally valuable expression of cultural creativity in the IOR. I have argued that UNESCO, the islands' politicians, tourism discourse and the historical elite produce their own discursive voicework which operates in the public space. It could be that some of this voicework is well meaning, since there is an astonishingly rapid 'loss' of diversity in the world today. I have also suggested that scholarly disciplines produce particular accounts of spaces in the IOR and that some of these have muted the islanders' voices/voicework. A third proposal has been that the islanders themselves, in their villages, on beaches, in cultural centers and homes have produced a profoundly rich voicework that enables innuendo, joking, the expression of ambivalent metaphors and transgressive bodily expression. In Sega, one's face must be able to quickly express both grief and mischief. Sega is a source of bodily strain (in the flexibility and facial expression required) and a means to shift the unbearable heaviness of being in an oppressive world. Voicework facilitates an imaginative lightness and verbal elusiveness.

To offer a final but important reflection, voicework is mutually and politically implicating. A local anthropologist such as myself is perhaps more open to and aware of the multidimensionality of voicework in these islands, not only because I speak the languages but also because I have residual social knowledge and I have been introduced to the analytical/northerly world of anthropology. However, as someone who has spent some time doing fieldwork in unequal societies, I am also aware of hegemonic discourses and how disciplines discipline the mind, producing particular ways of engaging with the world, often to the detriment of Other ways of doing so. In perceiving Sega as voicework in the IOR, I am proposing that scholars shift their senses somewhat to consider the thoroughly embedded and thus unique social world they are researching in the IOR. I have found it to be a rich, complex and multi-layered world in which voice plays a fundamental role in social expression. African descendants there, would benefit from being heard, deeply.

Notes

1. A concept used in the performance literature to represent the diverse performative uses of the (human) body for channeling discourses of power, hegemonies and sensualities.
2. Inaugural Lecture, Professor Andre Mukheibir, Nelson Mandela Metropolitan University, 2016.
3. Three Sega Legends from Mauritius in Sydney, https://www.youtube.com/watch?v=SZXxrmnVkl8 accessed 3 September 2016.
4. His local and formal name differs because in those villages where Creoles predominate, locals tend not share their local name (*ti noms*) with strangers. There is a belief that one's local name should be safeguarded by one's friends and family, since strangers may have nefarious intentions. Local names facilitated a network of tightly knit people who know each other well. One could depend on this network for defense in times of trouble.
5. Roger Clency, 'Bal ran Zarico', https://www.youtube.com/watch?v=7x3uT5cVDBc accessed 1 September 2016.
6. Serge Lebrasse, 'Moi mo ene ti Creole', https://www.youtube.com/watch?v=WhNUhXZkOps accessed 2 September 2016.
7. Louise, Joseph, 'Ti Kreol Leo', https://www.youtube.com/watch?v=RqeRdVwo_TQ accessed 7 September 2016.

8. Tonpa Documentary, https://www.youtube.com/watch?v=z0fze1noLoc accessed 10 September 2016.
9. Nancy Derougere, 'Laké Poilon', https://www.youtube.com/watch?v=CByz4W65-lk accessed 1 September 2016.
10. Marie-Josee Clency, 'Reprans mo Mari Anglais', https://www.youtube.com/watch?v=oyh5SzKB4Qk accessed 1 September 2016.
11. There seemed to have been a similar sentiment among Mauritian women after the war. Many women had 'moved on' to other partners and families, believing that their husbands would never return.
12. Voicescape is also linguistic. In Zanzibar though, several words triggered memory of an old Sega by Serge Lebrasse, entitled *Mo capitaine*, in which the singer asks a beautiful girl, where she is going. He says *'hapana wapi? Mo zoli sana?'* Half of the sentence is Swahili.

Disclosure statement

No potential conflict of interest was reported by the author.

References

Abu-Lughod, L. (1991). Writing against culture. In R. Fox (Ed.), *Recapturing anthropology: Working in the present* (pp. 466–479). Sante Fe: School of American Research Press.
Allen, R. (2001). Licentious and unbridled proceedings: The illegal slave trade to Mauritius and the Seychelles during the early 19th century. *Journal of African History, 42*(1), 91–116.
Alpers, E. (2000). Indian Ocean Africa: The island factor. *Emergences, 10*(2), 373–86.
Asad, T. (1979). *Anthropology and the colonial encounter*. London: Ithaca.
Bhabha, H. K. (1994). *The location of culture*. London: Routledge.
Boswell, R. (2006). *Le Malaise Creole: Ethnic identity in Mauritius*. Oxford: Berghahn Books.
Boswell, R. (2016). Bodybuilding as identity in South Africa. *African Identities, 14*(4), 384–395.
Boswell, R., & Nyamnjoh, F. (in press). *Postcolonial African anthropologies*. Pretoria: HSRC Press.
Bull, M., & Back, L. (2003). *The auditory culture reader*. Oxford: Berg.
Campbell, G. (1988). Slavery and Fanompoana: The structure of forced labour in Imerina (Madagascar), 1790-1861. *The Journal of African History, 29*(3): 463–486.
Clifford, J., & Marcus, G. (1986). *Writing culture: The poetics and politics of ethnography*. London: University of California Press.
Collen, L. (1995). *The rape of Sita*. London: Heinemann.
Depelchin, J. (2005). *Silences in African history: Between syndromes of discovery and abolition*. Dar Es Salaam: Mkuki Na Nyota.
Gill, R., Henwood, K., & Maclean, C. (2005). *Body projects and the regulation of normative masculinity*. London: LSE Research Articles Online.
Gimlin, D. (2007). What is body work? A review of the literature. *Sociology Compass, 1*, 350–370.

Ghosh, A. (2011). *River of Smoke*. London: John Murray.

Graeber, D. (2007). *Lost people: Magic and the legacy of slavery in Madagascar*. Bloomington: Indiana University Press.

Gurnah, A. (2001). *By the Sea*. London: Bloomsbury.

Haring, L. (2002). African folklore and creolization in the Indian Ocean islands. *Research in African Literatures, 33*(3), 182–199.

Haring, L. (2004). *Verbal art in Madagascar: Performance in historical perspective*. Philadelphia: University of Pennsylvania Press.

Hastrup, K. (1995). *A passage to anthropology: Between experience and theory*. Oxford: Routledge.

Hendy, D. (2013). *Noise*. New York, NY: Harper Collins.

Hoschild, A. R. (1979). *Emotion work, feeling rules, and social structure*. Retrieved from https://campus. fsu.edu/bbcswebdav/institution/academic/social_sciences/sociology/Reading%20Lists/Social% 20Psych%20Prelim%20Readings/II.%20Emotions/1979%20Hochschild%20-%20Emotion%2

Howes, D. (2010). *Hearing scents, tasting sights: toward a cross-cultural, multi-modal theory of aes- thetics. In F. Bacci, & D. Melcher (Eds.), Art and the senses* (pp. 161–182). Oxford: Oxford: University Press.

Jeffrey, L. (2007). How a plantation became a paradise: Changing representations of the homeland among displaced Chagos Islanders. *Journal of the Royal Anthropological Institute, 13*, 951–968.

Mafeje, A. (1996). *Anthropology and independent Africans: Suicide or end of an era?* Dakar: Codesria.

Mascia-Lewis, F. (2013). *A companion to the anthropology of the body and embodiment*. London: Wiley-Blackwell.

Moore, H. (1994). *A passion for difference: Essays in anthropology and gender*. Indiana: University Press.

Naipaul, V.S. (1972). *The Overcrowded Barracoon*. London: Penguin

Nyamnjoh, F., & Fuh, D. (2014). Africans-consuming-hair-africans-consumed-by-hair. *Africa Insight, 44*, 52–68.

Ramamonjisoa, S. (2001). Rituels ancestraux, les cultes de la vie et la recherche de l'harmonie. In *Madagascar Fenêtres* (pp. 18–31). Antananarivo: Cité.

Randrianja, S., & Ellis, S. (2009). *Madagascar, A short history*. London: Hurst & Company.

Salverda, T. (2015). *The Franco-Mauritian elite: Power and anxiety in the face of change*. Oxford: Berghahn.

Sharp, L. (1995). Playboy Princely spirits of Madagascar: Possession as youthful commentary and social critique. *Anthropological Quarterly 68*(2), 75–88.

Sharp, L. (2001). *The Possessed and the dispossessed: Spirits, power and identity in a Madagascar migrant town*. UCLA: Berkeley.

Shell, R. (1994). *Children of bondage: A social history of the slave society at the Cape of Good Hope, 1652-1838*. London: Wesleyan Press.

Sheriff, A. (1987). *Slaves, spices and Ivory in Zanzibar*. London: James Currey.

Spivak, G. (1988). Can the subaltern speak? In C. Nelson, & L. Grossberg (Eds.), *Marxism and the interpretation of culture* (pp. 271–313). Urbana: University of Illinois Press.

Tate, S. (2015). *Black women's bodies and the state: Race, gender and culture*. London: Macmillan.

Teelock, V. (1998). *Bitter sugar, sugar and slavery in 19th century Mauritius*. Réduit: Mahatma Gandhi Institute.

Van Wolputte, S. (2004). Hang on to yourself: Of bodies, embodiment, and selves. *Annual Review of Anthropology, 33*, 251–269.

Ward, K., & Worden, N. (1998). Commemorating, suppressing and invoking cape slavery. In S. Nuttall, & C. Coetzee (Eds.), *Negotiating the past: The making of memory in South Africa* (pp. 221–241). Cape Town: Oxford University Press.

Weidman, A. (2014). Anthropology and voice. *Annual Review of Anthropology, 43*, 37–51.

Women's economic empowerment in the Indian Ocean region through gender equality in work: building a common agenda

Priya Chacko

Introduction

Women's economic empowerment (WEE) can be defined as the process of change that gives women (i) access to and control over resources and markets; (ii) increased agency and choice and; (iii) the capacity to improve and control specific outcomes or achievements (such as enhanced well-being and dignity and improved economic opportunities); and (iv) the ability to influence the wider policy, regulatory and institutional environment (WIEGO, 2016). Improving women's labor force participation has long been seen as key to WEE. However, the vast majority of the world's women, including in the Indian Ocean region, face significant challenges in entering the labor market, and if they succeed in doing so, are likely to work in low-paid jobs with little access to social protections. Hence, increased labor force participation may not necessarily lead to substantive poverty reduction but may, indeed, entrench poverty (UNIFEM, 2005, p. 19).

This paper argues that WEE should be placed high on the agenda of the Indian Ocean Rim Association (IORA), with a focus on improving the conditions of women's labor force participation to achieve gender equality in work, which can be defined as the 'ability of women to find employment and be compensated fairly for it, share unpaid care work equitably, have the skills and opportunity to perform higher-productivity jobs, and occupy leadership positions' (McKinsey Global Institute, 2015, p. 42). A significant hurdle in building a common agenda for IORA is the socio-economic diversity of countries in the region. All countries of the region, however, face significant challenges in the area of women's labor force participation. The majority of female workers in the Indian Ocean region, in both developed and developing countries, are engaged in precarious work through non-standard forms and self-employment in both the formal (regulated) economy and informal (unregulated) economy. While not all workers in non-standard forms of employment and self-employment face economic insecurity, research shows that the majority of such workers often have diminished or no access to legal and social protections and therefore experience significant economic uncertainty (ILO, 2013, 2016a). Finding ways to overcome these challenges should become not just a focus of consultations between officials and civil society leaders, but a means of facilitating people-to-people links through the sharing of experiences and strategies for securing better social and legal protections for female workers.

In this respect, IORA can learn from other regional organisations but it can also be a pioneer in the use of Track Three processes to facilitate WEE.

This paper seeks to first outline the economic and welfare benefits of gender equality in work. It then identifies key challenges to the achievement of gender equality in work, in general, and in the Indian Ocean region, in particular, and ends by making key recommendations.

WEE through gender equality in work

The correlation between WEE, women's welfare and economic growth has been recognized by IORA, which notes on its website: 'Empowering women and girls is regarded as an essential part of the solution to some of the most serious global challenges of today: food security, poverty reduction and sustainable development' (IORA, 2016). There remains significant global disparity between men and women's labor force participation. In 2015, 50% of women of working age were in paid employment compared to 77% of men. These rates have remained roughly stagnant since 1995 (UN, 2015, p. 89). This disparity has major costs. A recent McKinsey report, for instance, has shown that if gender parity in labor markets were to be achieved, this would add as much as $28 trillion or 26% to the global annual gross domestic product (GDP) in 2025. Even improvements in gender parity in each state to match the rate of improvement in best-performing countries in their particular regions would add $12 trillion to the GDP in 2025 (McKinsey Global Institute, 2015, p. 1). Countries within the Indian Ocean region would gain the most from improvements in gender parity in labor force participation. India, for instance, would experience a 16% increase in GDP, while the rest of South Asia, the Middle East and North Africa and Oceania would each benefit by 11% and South East Asia would benefit by 8% in 2025 (McKinsey Global Institute, 2015).

Gender equality in work, defined as the 'ability of women to find employment and be compensated fairly for it, share unpaid care work equitably, have the skills and opportunity to perform higher-productivity jobs, and occupy leadership positions', is a key component of gender parity and poverty reduction (McKinsey Global Institute, 2015, p. 42). Yet in both developed and developing countries globally, female workers are predominantly engaged in non-standard forms of employment and self-employment. The growth of such forms of employment constitutes a significant challenge to gender equality in work. As the International Labour Organization defines it, non-standard forms of employment 'covers work that falls outside the scope of a standard employment relationship, which itself is understood as being work that is full-time, indefinite employment in a subordinate employment relationship' (ILO, 2016a, pp. 1–2). This includes temporary, casual and fixed-term employment, temporary agency work and other contractual arrangements involving multiple parties, ambiguous employment relationships and part-time employment. Non-standard forms of employment occur in both formal and informal working arrangements in a subordinate employment relationship. Informal working arrangements typically exclude access to formal contracts, national labor laws, employment benefits and social protections. Self-employment is particularly prevalent in the informal sector, and includes a range of occupations including home-based workers, street vendors and waste pickers (UNIFEM, 2005, p. 39). Contrary to predictions in the 1970s, informal employment has continued to grow due, in particular, to changes in the global political economy. It now constitutes a significant share of the global economy and labor force, and informal employment is the major source of employment for women in developing countries. Non-standard forms of employment in the formal sector and self-employment are also increasing (ILO, 2016a, p. 3).

Non-standard forms of employment and self-employment do offer some benefits for workers, such as flexible working hours and lower input costs. However, the costs of non-standard forms of employment and self-employment can be significant. The growth of non-standard employment deepens labor market segmentation, in which 'non-regular' workers experience insecure and inferior working and bear the brunt of economic crises (ILO, 2016a, p. 32). Workers in non-standard forms of employment and self-employment often lack full access to the social protections offered to workers in standard employment, such as leave provisions, healthcare and pension benefits (ILO, 2016a, pp. 26–27). They also lack access to training opportunities, have a higher rate of accidents at work and experience adverse health outcomes as a result of job insecurity (ILO, 2016a, pp. 28–29). Studies have shown a significant overlap between poverty and employment in the informal economy, in which female self-employment flourishes, with workers earning lower hourly wages, having less job security and being at a higher risk of falling into poverty (ILO, 2016a; UN, 2015, pp. 104–105). Self-employment in the formal economy includes consultants, professionals and contractors in the services sector as well as small-business owners. Self-employment is associated with significant income disparities between men and women and low incomes for women, owing in part to the fewer hours worked by women. In OECD countries, the gap in median earnings between self-employed men and women is 30–40%, compared to 16% in the case of salaried jobs (OECD, 2012, p. 6).

Reasons for the concentration of women in non-standard forms of employment and self-employment

Unpaid care work

Women's unpaid care work, in particular, represents a significant constraint on gender equality in work. Women's greater responsibility for care work is shaped by social norms and is worsened by low public spending on social services and demographic trends toward aging populations (UNIFEM, 2005, pp. 25–26). Currently 75% of unpaid care work globally, including child care, caring for the elderly, cooking and cleaning, is undertaken by women leading to either exclusion from the labor market or a greater proportion of women than men undertaking part-time or casual work (McKinsey Global Institute, 2015, p. 2). The McKinsey report estimates that increasing labor force participation accounts for 54% of potential global GDP growth while closing the gap between hours worked between men and women accounts for 23% of potential GDP growth (McKinsey Global Institute, 2015, p. 4). Reductions in the time women spend on unpaid care work not only increase GDP by increasing labour force participation rates, but also lead to greater financial independence and the potential to attain training for higher-productivity work. It can also have intergenerational benefits since research has shown that daughters of working women are more likely to undertake paid employment, with higher earnings and better quality jobs (McKinsey Global Institute, 2015, p. 30).

The nature of contemporary job creation

In both developed and developing countries, in recent decades, employment growth has been in non-standard forms of employment such as temporary, fixed-term and part-time contracts, which are not, in general, conducive to gender parity or poverty reduction (UNIFEM, 2005, p. 55). In developing countries, for instance, economic growth has been produced through the establishment of export processing zones and global value changes that utilize centralized production practices, contractors and industrial out-workers. These forms of production are volatile, cyclical and depend on the weak bargaining power of workers for profits. Women have been more likely than men to be employed in such forms of production because of the premium placed on low-skilled and low-paid workers (ILO, 2016a, p. 71). In developed countries, also, non-standard forms of employ-ment have been increasing. In some parts of the world this is due to concerted govern-ment policy to address the work–life balance (ILO, 2016a, p. 15). However, it is mostly due to economic crises and changes in hiring practices of firms for cost advantages and flexibility (ILO, 2016a, pp. 3–4). In addition, government initiatives for poverty alleviation and growth have increasingly focused on promoting enterprise development, particularly for micro, small and medium-sized enterprises (SMEs), on the basis that entrepreneurship can raise incomes and empower individuals and communities (Goulding, 2013, p. 29). Hence, increasing self-employment has become a target of government policies.

Social norms, legal limitations and educational inequality

Social norms that lead to gender stereotypes about women's right and propensity to work outside the home contribute to limitations and greater insecurity in women's employ-ment. The view, for instance, that women's income is secondary to the 'male breadwinner' means that women are often the first to be dismissed from continuing employment and therefore enter into more precarious non-standard forms of employment or self-employ-ment (Goulding, 2013, p. 9). While all countries have ratified the Convention on the Elim-ination of All Forms of Discrimination against Women (CEDAW), gender stereotypes continue to pervade recruitment practices and wage systems because of unclear national legislation as to the scope of discrimination and weak enforcement procedures, jurispru-dence or methods of conciliation and arbitration to address disputes (Goulding, 2013, p. 18). This contributes to wage differentials between similarly qualified men and women and obstacles to career advancement, such as a shift into managerial or supervi-sory roles. Social norms and discrimination are also associated with limiting women's access to education. Access to higher education and skills training is associated with raising women's labour force participation and better quality employment. Moreover, women with parity in education are more likely to share unpaid care work equitably, be employed in professional and technical occupation and assume leadership positions (McKinsey Global Institute, 2015).

Female labour force participation in the Indian Ocean region

Gender-disaggregated data are not readily available for all countries in the Indian Ocean region; however, the available data suggest that global trends in the quality of female labor market participation are reflected and sometimes amplified in the Indian Ocean region. In most countries of the region, women make up significantly less than half of the workforce. In some states, such as India, female labor force participation is in decline and this can only partly be explained by women choosing to undertake longer periods of education (Ghosh, 2015, p. 49). The available data show that women spend a much larger amount of time on unpaid care work. Australia, for instance, lies in the top four OECD countries for unpaid care work inequality with women spending almost double the amount of time on unpaid work as men. Part-time work for women is common in Australia and accounted for 45% of women's employment, compared to 15% of men's employment, in 2007 (Abhayaratna, Andrews, Nuch, & Podbury, 2008, p. xviii). Care responsibilities are the most common reason cited by women of prime working age for entering part-time employment (Abhayaratna et al., 2008, p. xxiii). In India, National Sample Surveys show that 93% of women report being involuntarily compelled to stay out of the labor force because of their care responsibilities. Of these women, 30% would like to be employed on a full-time or part-time basis (UN Women, 2015, p. 11).

Existing data suggest that slightly more women than men in the Indian Ocean region work in the informal economy and all but one country, Thailand, has higher female poverty rates than male poverty rates (UN Women, 2015, pp. 9, 12). Non-standard forms of employment and self-employment are prevalent in the region. About 43% of women in the region are self-employed and most work in the informal economy (UN Women, 2015, p. 17). As mentioned above, part-time employment is prevalent in some countries like Australia. Several countries in the region have policies in place designed to facilitate borrowing for microenterprises and SMEs, however, the evidence for the impact of such measures on poverty reduction, a reduction in unpaid care work and economic autonomy is very mixed (Garikipati, 2013). Areas that have been identified as key for economic growth and integration in the Indian Ocean region include tourism and fisheries. The nature of female labor force participation in these sectors, however, does not bode well for the achievement of gender equality in work. Women's employment in fisheries in the Indian Ocean region, for instance, tends to be concentrated in informal, low-paid jobs related to seafood processing without access to labour or social protections (Harper, Zeller, Hauzer, Pauly, & Sumaila, 2013, p. 57). Likewise, women make up about 49% of the workforce in the tourism industry globally (UN Women, 2010, p. ii). However, women tend to occupy clerical and service jobs such as retail, cleaning and cooking. The majority of workers in non-standard forms of employment in tourism are women and they contribute significantly to unpaid work in family-run tourism enterprises. On average, it is estimated that women earn 10–15% less than male workers in tourism (Ferguson, 2011, p. 238; UN Women, 2010, p. ii). Without concerted policy changes to address the gendered aspects of the fishery and tourism industries that are detrimental to female workers, and without the provision of better labor and social protections for women workers, a focus on fisheries development and tourism will not lead to WEE in any meaningful way and may even exacerbate inequalities.

Gender stereotypes, educational inequality and legal restrictions and limitations that inhibit women's labor force participation are widespread in the Indian Ocean region. Research on Bangladesh, for instance, has shown that among the major factors that restrict career advancement for women are perceptions among managers of women's inferior capabilities and sexual harassment. Similar perceptions have been found to mar career advancement for women in South Africa (UN Women, 2015, p. 14). Strong links have been found between attitudes that place limitations on women and low labor force partici- pation in key parts of the Indian Ocean region like South Asia, the Middle East and North Africa (McKinsey Global Institute, 2015, p. 14). Significant limitations continue to exist in the region with respect to legal institutions that ensure gender equality at work by preventing gender discrimination and equal remuneration (UN Women, 2015, pp. 5, 24). Moreover, on average, the available data show that only 7.4% of women in the Indian Ocean region have a secondary or higher education, which is half that of the rate of men (UN Women, 2015, p. 21). Gender differentiation in tertiary education in terms of subjects studied continues to be prevalent in the region with women predomi- nantly pursuing studies in Arts and Humanities rather than science, engineering, manufac- turing and construction, which are generally associated with higher incomes and work opportunities (UN Women, 2015, pp. 22–23).

Conclusion and recommendations

There are a number of possible interventions that could be undertaken to achieving gender equality in work in the Indian Ocean rim region. The precise nature of interventions will of course depend on the country-specific context. Reducing the burden of unpaid care work on women, for instance, requires public policy interventions to give women access to labor-saving appliances, child care and palliative care for elderly relatives (ILO, 2016b, pp. 78–88). Increased social investment in the care economy has the potential to create a 'virtuous cycle' of reducing unpaid care work, formal job creation in care work, increasing women's labor force participation and economic growth (ILO, 2016b, p. 89). Also necessary is the provision of family and parental leave and advocacy to change social norms regard- ing men and women's responsibility for unpaid care work (McKinsey Global Institute, 2015, p. 21). Considering the size of the informal economy in the Indian Ocean region and the trends in job creation, achieving gender equality in work will require strengthening social protections for workers in non-standard forms of employment and self-employment. Legal reforms are necessary to strengthen anti-discrimination laws and educational reforms are needed to increase access to secondary and higher education. Perhaps most importantly, however, none of these reforms and interventions are likely to be achieved without giving female workers and their representative bodies access to policy-making processes.

Hence, achieving gender equality in work will require policy, legal and regulatory changes and the social and political empowerment of women workers so that they can seek and achieve improvements in the social, political and economic structures that con- tribute to inequality. There is significant diversity among countries in the Indian Ocean region with regard to the extent of women's economic, social and political empowerment, however, as this paper has shown, all countries in the region, whether developed or devel- oping, face significant challenges in achieving gender equality in work. The economic and welfare benefits of WEE through gender equality in work, however, are clear and numer- ous. This paper makes the following recommendations:

(1) IORA should prioritize the collection of gender-disaggregated data on women's labor force participation in the Indian Ocean region to inform national and regional policy- making

While sufficient data are available to give a broad picture of women's labor force participation in the Indian Ocean region, there is lack of comparable and comprehensive
gender-disaggregated data which can be used to inform national and regional policy-
making. The absence of such data is a major constraint to improving gender equity and
must be a priority for IORA.

(2) Track Two processes should be established to deliver gender-sensitive policy advice
     related to job creation programs and regional economic integration initiatives

Other multilateral organizations and regional groups such as the Group of 20 (G20) and
Asia Pacific Economic Cooperation (APEC) forum have created working groups to specifically focus on issues of gender equality. APEC, for instance, has formed the Private-Public
Dialogue on Women and the Economy. This grouping focuses specifically on issues of WEE
in order to increase the inclusion of women in the regional economy and 'elevate the influence of women's issues within APEC' (APEC, 2016). This is an approach that also be
adopted by IORA to maintain a consistent focus on gender equality in national and
regional policy making.

(3) Track Three processes should be established to facilitate links between women
     workers and their representative organizations in the Indian Ocean region so that col-
     lective action strategies and experiences can be shared

Gender equality at work can only be facilitated by the social and political empowerment of
women which ensures access to legal and social protections, such as laws against discrimination, education, health care, childcare and social protection. There is considerable variation between and within states in the region as to the types of protections women
workers enjoy. For instance, in India, informal workers in some states, such as Tamil
Nadu, have successfully mobilized to obtain social protections from the regional government (Agarwala, 2013). The sharing of such experiences can be a productive way of deepening people-to-people links in the region while also promoting WEE.

References

Abhayaratna, J., Andrews, L., Nuch, H., & Podbury, T. (2008). *Part-time employment: The Australian
experience*. Melbourne: Productivity Commission.
Agarwala, R. (2013). *Informal labor, formal politics, and dignified discontent in India*. Cambridge:
Cambridge University Press.
APEC. (2016). Policy partnership on women and the economy. APEC. Retrieved August 30, from
http://www.apec.org/Groups/SOM-Steering-Committee-on-Economic-and-Technical-
Cooperation/Working-Groups/Policy-Partnership-on-Women-and-the-Economy.aspx
Ferguson, L. (2011). Promoting gender equality and empowering women? Tourism and the third mil-
lennium development goal. *Current Issues in Tourism, 14*(3), 235–249.

Garikipati, S. (2013). Microcredit and women's empowerment: Have we been looking at the wrong indicators? *Oxford Development Studies, 41*(suppl. 1), S53–S75.

Ghosh, J. (2015). Growth, industrialisation and inequality in India. *Journal of the Asia Pacific Economy, 20*(1), 42–56.

Goulding, K. (2013). *Gender dimensions of national employment policies: A 24 country study.* Geneva: International Labour Organization.

Harper, S., Zeller, D., Hauzer, M., Pauly, D., & Sumaila, U. R. (2013). Women and fisheries: Contribution to food security and local economies. *Marine Policy, 39*, 56–63.

ILO. (2013). *Non-standard forms of employment: Report for discussion at the meeting of experts on non-standard forms of employment.* Geneva: International Labour Organization.

ILO. (2016a). Non-standard forms of employment. International Labour Organization. Retrieved August 29, from http://www.ilo.org/global/topics/employment-security/non-standard-employment/lang--en/index.htm

ILO. (2016b). *Women at work: Trends* 2016. Geneva: International Labour Organization.

IORA. (2016). Gender Empowerment. IORA. Retrieved August 30, from http://www.iora.net/about-us/priority-areas/gender-empowerment.aspx

McKinsey Global Institute. (2015). *The power of parity: How advancing women's equality can add $12 trillion to global growth.* McKinsey & Company. Retrieved from http://www.mckinsey.com/global-themes/employment-and-growth/how-advancing-womens-equality-can-add-12-trillion-to-global-growth

OECD. (2012). *Gender equality in education, employment and entrepreneurship: Final report to the MCM 2012.* OECD. Retrieved from https://www.oecd.org/employment/50423364.pdf

UN. (2015). *The world's women 2015: Trends and statistics.* Geneva: United Nations.

UNIFEM. (2005). *Progress of the world's women 2005: Women, work and poverty.* New York, NY: United Nations Development Fund.

UN Women. (2010). *Global report on women in tourism* 2010. New York: United Nations.

UN Women. (2015). *Enabling women's contributions to the Indian Ocean Rim economies.* New York: United Nations.

WIEGO. (2016). Women's Economic Empowerment: WIEGO Position and Approach. WIEGO. Retrieved August 30, from http://wiego.org/sites/wiego.org/files/resources/files/Chen_EconomicEmpowerment_WIEGO_Position.pdf

Women's empowerment in the global South

Women's empowerment in South Asia: NGO interventions and agency building in Bangladesh, by Pranab Panday, London and New York, Routledge, 2016, 110 pp., £90, ISBN 978-1-138-94370-4

Education, gender and development: A capability perspective, by Mari-Anne Okkolin, London and New York, Routledge, 2017, 258 pp., £90, ISBN 978-1-138-67304-5

The relation between women's empowerment and development, understood either as economic or human development, continues to be the object of much academic work. The two books reviewed here are part of this ongoing interest, but they also point to an area that deserves particular attention: women's voices. The interest in people's voices in development studies can be traced back to the effort of the World Bank to collect the experiences of the poor, published in three separate volumes, known as the 'Voices of the Poor.' These voices have been typically used to illustrate the challenges associated with the design and implementation of development policies, programs and projects in the global South. There is no denying the value of such an approach. However, something is lost when we focus on the barriers to development. These books showcase that studying enabling factors can enrich our understanding of the relation between empowerment and development in the global South.

The two books share important similarities. They both explore and recount stories of women's empowerment in contexts shaped by material limitations, patriarchal structures, and cultural constraints. They deploy qualitative approaches in the form of in-depth interviews, but they also provide quantitative data that adds strength to their findings and helps ground their studies in the broader national and global contexts. They both adopt the 'gender and development' (GAD) approach rather than the 'women in development' (WID) approach. In this sense, Panday notes how women's participation in politics alone (a WID approach) does not translate automatically into empowerment. Instead, a full account of the gender dynamics (a GAD approach) is necessary to assess women's political agency. In a similar vein, Okkolin notes how gender parity in education (a WID approach) is not enough to understand the full impact of education on women's agency. Instead, this requires examining the broader dynamics of gender equality and inequality (a GAD approach). In this sense, both authors note how gender roles and images of womanhood linked to the domestic/private sphere (e.g. marriage, family, childcare) constrain women's agency (i.e. their choices and their capacity to act upon those choices). Interestingly, their research also reveals how men (e.g. fathers, husbands, friends, colleagues) can be important enabling factors in the educational, social and political empowerment of women in the global South. Both studies adopt and adapt the capabilities approach associated with the work of Amartya Sen, and embrace the concept of human development championed by the United Nations Development Programme. Last but not least, they both position women's voices as central to their analyses of women's agency and empowerment in the global South.

Yet, for all their similarities, there are also important differences, not least in the execution of the task. Thus, whilst Okkolin's book is an outstanding contribution to the field, Panday's contribution, whilst interesting and valuable, comes across as a missed opportunity.

Pranab Panday's *Women's empowerment in South Asia* is a short study of the contribution made by non-governmental organizations (NGOs) in empowering women through agency building in Bangladesh. The book identifies factors that motivate women to become active participants in development projects, explores factors that enable them to serve their communities, identifies major barriers to women's participation (i.e. established institutions and traditional customs), and suggests strategies to overcome such barriers. But above all, the book is a vindication of the impact that Sharique, a Swiss NGO, has had on women's empowerment and political participation in Bangladesh.

The book is structured in seven chapters, which can be broadly divided in two parts. The first three chapters introduce the main themes (Chapter 1), discuss conceptual issues and set up the theoretical framework (Chapter 2), and provide a brief account of NGOs in Bangladesh (Chapter 3). The remaining chapters analyze the extent of women's participation in community activities (Chapter 4), the impact of Sharique's intervention on women's lives at the community level (Chapter 5), and on women's status at the institutional level (Chapter 6). The book concludes with some lessons learned from Sharique's work in Bangladesh.

The contextual and conceptual chapters, whilst informative and interesting, lack the level of rigor and clarity one should expect in a published manuscript. Panday brings up a range of closely related concepts, such as participation, empowerment, capabilities, and agency. However, the construction of the theoretical framework is rather clunky, and the relationship between the different concepts is not clearly articulated. Thus, for example, just before empowerment is defined as an outcome, that is, an expansion of agency (p. 29), agency is referred to as a means of empowerment (p. 28). The lack of clarity and rigor is also exemplified by the treatment of the four elements of empowerment (assets, knowledge, will and capacity) adopted from the work of Charlier, Caubergs with Malpas, and Kakiba (2007). Panday repeatedly refers to these four elements as indicators. This can only be described as a categorical error, or at the very least categorical confusion, since Charlier et al. (2007) use assets, knowledge, will and capacity as elements (or aspects) of empowerment, not as indicators. Indicators are features that can be measured so as to determine the extent to which those elements are present (e.g. income is an indicator of assets, level of education is an indicator of knowledge, etc.). Having said that, as we shall see later, one of the most interesting aspects of Panday's book derives from his engagement with the 'women empowerment approach' developed by Charlier et al. (2007).

The quality of the book is also undermined by a wide range of errors. Thus, for example, the Preface states that, at present, 50 seats out of a total of 350 are reserved for women in the national parliament of Bangladesh (p. xii), whilst in the Introduction those figures are 45 seats of a total of 345 (p. 2). There is a significant number of proofing errors: 'potential gaps are which a project' (p. 4), 'something that is achieves the ways' (p. 21), 'Sharique participation rates than those from control areas' (p. 54), 'their localitiesy' (p. 65), 'the main purpose of this is be to analyse' (p. 83). There is also a common (but unforgivable at this level) reference to Africa as a country (p. 27); and there is a call for further research of the role of NGOs based on a source from 1987 (p. 39).

Panday's work, however, adds value to our understanding of women's empowerment in the global South. The most interesting part of this contribution lies in the second part of the book, when the author analyzes the impact of Sharique's programs. The way in which the author sets up the research project, using 'control groups' against which to measure the impact of Sharique's programs, is interesting and strengthens the analysis and the conclusions. Yet the analysis could be better contextualized. For one thing, the author, whilst providing a brief and superficial engagement with the role on NGOs in a neoliberal context (Chapter 2), makes no comment about the imposition of global North agendas on the global South. In other words, some contextualization of the role of Sharique in the global North versus global South tension would have been useful. Moreover, the integration of Sharique into the narrative is clunky to say the least. The NGO appears abruptly on page 43. Panday simply states that 'The third phase of the Sharique project started in September 2013.' But what is Sharique? And what were the first and second phases of the Sharique project? The answer to the second question is nowhere to be found. The best answer to the first question is in a footnote on page 62: 'SHARIQUE means "Partnership." It is a Swiss Development Cooperation (SDC) funded local governance project that is working for establishing accountable, transparent and inclusive local governance in Bangladesh.'

The most interesting finding derived from this study is the replacing of assets with knowledge as the first step in the empowerment process. Panday argues that knowledge brings about change in assets, which in turn enables women's willpower, and as their will becomes stronger, their capacity increases, allowing them to influence the decision-making process, including their ability to make decisions for themselves and for others. In short, knowledge is presented as the key to kick-start women's empowerment and enhance their political agency. Positioning knowledge as the starting point serves to vindicate (or perhaps reflects) the role of Sharique in building women's empowerment in Bangladesh. Significantly, this poses a direct challenge to the framework created by Charlier et al. (2007), and carries potential implications for further research. Indeed, this argument could present an important contribution to our understanding of empowerment in the global South. However, the author does not push the implications of that conclusion, and even presents this in a somewhat casual fashion, simply stating: 'I think that the first step is knowledge' (p. 27). I think he might be right, but I also think the way the research was presented in this book was a missed opportunity to make a much stronger claim and a more substantive contribution to our understanding of women's empowerment in the global South.

The best chapter of the book is Chapter 5. Not only is this where the voices of women finally appear in the text, but this also where we can see the transformation of women's lives. More than any other, this chapter is the one that validates the research project and vindicates the intervention of Sharique in the lives of women in Bangladesh. The fact that the women make explicit references to how Sharique's programs have empowered them is the most powerful evidence and vindication of their work in Bangladesh. Yet it is also at this stage that the most disappointing aspect of this text is revealed. I refer to the way in which the author presents the evidence gathered through the in-depth interviews. The actual voices of the women are barely heard! Panday uses 'case studies' to illustrate how the women have benefitted from their engagement with Sharique. However, the author reports on these cases through short biographical summaries, with barely any words from the participants. The first quote of a statement by one of the women does not appear until page 60, and the first mention of Sharique by one of the women in a quoted statement appears in page 71.

This presentation of the material is somewhat inconsistent with a text that takes voice as central to the story of women's empowerment. Giving space to those voices would have required a lot more work, and perhaps a different structure, one that gave more space to the articulations of agency by the women themselves, in their own words. Given the brevity of this text (just over 100 pages), space was certainly not an issue here. The significant number of interviews conducted for this project suggests that this research could have been turned into a more substantial (and longer) monograph. The fact that many voices were recorded but few statements were shared comes across as a missed opportunity – particularly when contrasted with the other text reviewed here.

Mari-Anne Okkolin's *Education, gender and development* is a masterful display of academic scholarship. The book takes a novel approach to female education in the global South. Okkolin offers a fresh voice to the field of development studies, and does so largely by integrating the voices of women, effectively and systematically, into her study of female education in Tanzania. The book is a sophisticated, systematic and reflexive exercise, with a perfectly consistent alignment between the theoretical framework, the methodological approach, and the narrative articulation. Indeed, this is a book that deserves a wide academic readership, and one that needs to be read to be fully appreciated. The text can be used to teach graduates how to integrate theory, methodology and analysis in a way that is coherent, elegant and sophisticated.

The book is structured in three main parts, with the Conclusion listed as Part IV. Part I introduces the book (Chapter 1), the key themes (Chapter 2), the women (Chapter 3), and the empirical study (Chapter 4). Part II discusses the field of study (Chapter 5), explains the Tanzanian context (Chapter 6), and provides the theoretical framework (Chapter 7). Part III is the largest part and the core of the book. The three empirical chapters that form this part explore the women's school experiences (Chapter 8), social and familial experiences (Chapter 9), and agency notions (Chapter 10). The Conclusion sums up the findings, provides some additional reflections, and culminates with a telling statement from one of the participants: 'I'm happy.'

The book is rooted in the capabilities approach, particularly in the work of Amartya Sen and his emphasis on voice as central to human agency and development. Okkolin positions voice at the heart of the theoretical framework, but also as central to the methodological approach (e.g. the structure of the interviews and interactions with the participants) and the crafting of the narrative. The voice-centered relational method she uses requires and demands 'intensive listening, not only during the interview, but also at the time of reading and interpreting the interview transcripts' (p. 22). The author remains in control of the articulation of the analysis and the formulation of the argument, mapping the journey through the landscape of statements articulated by the participants. Yet, at the same time, Okkolin shows that those voices already contain most of the analysis. In other words, the author makes the participants analytical partners, and not mere subjects of study and analysis.

Okkolin operates with and deploys a reflexive understanding of 'the relational process of knowledge construction' (p. 37). The fact that she is aware that knowledge is always subjective, situated and partial, and that 'every research activity is an intervention' (p. 36), does not undermine her analysis (i.e. there is no sense of aporia or analysis paralysis) or weaken her conclusions. Instead, this approach allows her to present the insights derived from her research as a 'collaborative accomplishment' (p. 37). Thus, whilst the author guides the research process and our path through the landscape, the landscape itself is one that emerges from the stories of the 10 women interviewed in this project. Their voices dominate the second half of the book, and provide the final words. The book concludes with a well-organized collection of five statements from four of the participants. The statements emphasize equality of opportunities (the dominant frame of this study) and the value of education (the key theme of the book). The expressions of happiness in the two final statements capture perfectly the impact that education has had in the lives of these women, and do so in terms that are deeply personal, and almost existential: 'I'm happy.'

The focus on voice is linked directly to the other driving concept here: agency. Okkolin borrows the four variations of agency from Sen: well-being achievements (or functionings), well-being freedoms (or capabilities), agency achievements, and agency freedoms. The analysis provides a complex picture of agency and an overall narrative of empowerment, particularly as the participants move into secondary education. Indeed, Okkolin concludes that secondary education (not primary education) is the key to these women's educational empowerment. In this sense, her study resonates with and vindicates the findings from a recent review of the state of women's agency and empowerment in developing countries, which underlines the importance of going beyond primary schooling (Hanmer & Klugman, 2016).

The book explores a wide range of enabling and constraining factors that shape women's educational agency: physical, mental, social, familial, and learning environments. Okkolin identifies four kinds of capability freedoms to construct educational well-being and agency, based on the narratives of the participants: 'systemic given' (agency within the system), 'educated by someone' (agency within the family), 'own reasoning' (individual agency), and 'yes but no' (agency within ambivalence). In the final analysis, despite the structural and systemic constrains, and the limited opportunities and freedoms, the women reveal 'positive and emancipated ideas of themselves as agents in their own lives' (p. 215), viewing themselves as 'intentional, rational, agents, capable of justified evaluation and decision-making' who 'pursued what they saw as possible and realised the nearly impossible in the Tanzanian context' (p. 215).

Okkolin's book is, first and foremost, a study of female agency, that is, a study of the capacity and autonomy of the participants to make decisions and take actions regarding their educational choices. These decisions, actions and choices are circumscribed and contextualized by limited resources (although the participants identify as middle class), patriarchal structures (although several of the fathers are supportive of their daughters education), and cultural constraints (e.g. a particular conception of the idea of Tanzanian woman). The author explores the tension between agency and structure expertly and elegantly, and provides a nuanced and sophisticated story of female empowerment.

Interestingly, Okkolin hardly engages with the concept of empowerment, which she aptly defines as 'the expansion of agency' (p. 104). This seems to derive from the fact that, as the author notes, empowerment is not a term that the capabilities approach often employs. Thus, consistent with this, Okkolin states explicitly that the concept of empowerment is not applied in her book. Yet, it is impossible not to read her text as a narrative of women's empowerment. The book is an account of how education, most notably secondary education, and a range of factors that contribute to the success of these women in the education system (e.g. parental support, friendships, personal drive), empower women to make educational, social and professional choices throughout their lives.

Whilst there are no shortcomings in this text, there is an intriguing omission from the references, namely, Elinami Swai's book *Beyond women's empowerment in Africa* (2010). This book takes a very critical view of narratives of empowerment, in particular the notion of formal education as the path for women's empowerment in Africa. Swai argues that formal education, far from being a liberating and empowering tool, dislocates women and suppresses their creativity and agency by undermining (i.e. marginalizing and trivializing) so-called 'traditional' women's knowledge systems. This kind of knowledge, she argues, not only is central to women's agency, but sustains the African continent in a myriad of ways. The omission of this text is particularly intriguing because Swai's work focuses on Tanzania. I cannot but wonder whether Okkolin is aware of Swai's work and/or how would she react or respond to such a critical view of formal education. I wonder if her refusal to deploy empowerment as a concept in her study was a way to avoid engagement with Swai's work. This remains an intriguing question. In any case, it would have been fascinating to read Okkolin's defense of her analysis of formal education in terms of women's empowerment, and in relation to Swai's work on women's agency in Tanzania.

To conclude, irrespective of the marked contrast in the articulation of their findings, these two books vindicate the focus on gender in general and women's voices in particular in the study of development, both in terms of economic and human development, in the global South. Moreover, for all the contextual differences between the two countries studied here,

Bangladesh and Tanzania, there are shared (perhaps universal) elements to both stories and contexts: patriarchal structures that keep women 'in their place' and images on what constitutes a 'proper woman,' but also role models and champions (including male ones, particularly fathers) that contribute to challenge and/or overcome those images and structures. In the final analysis, these two books are useful resources for researchers (and practitioners) willing to listen to women's voices and understand women's roles in the ongoing process of women's empowerment and human development in the global South.

References

Charlier, S., Caubergs, L. with Malpas, N., & Kakiba, E. M. (2007). *The women empowerment approach: A methodological guide*. Brussels: Commission on Women and Development.

Hanmer, L., & Klugman, J. (2016). Exploring women's agency and empowerment in developing countries: Where do we stand? *Feminist Economics*, *22*(1), 237–263.

Swai, E. V. (2010). *Beyond women's empowerment in Africa: Exploring dislocation and agency*. New York, NY: Palgrave Macmillan.

Benito Cao

Index

Note: Page numbers in *italics* refer to figures
Page numbers in **bold** refer to tables

For Product Safety Concerns and Information please contact our EU
representative GPSR@taylorandfrancis.com
Taylor & Francis Verlag GmbH, Kaufingerstraße 24, 80331 München, Germany

www.ingramcontent.com/pod-product-compliance
Ingram Content Group UK Ltd.
Pitfield, Milton Keynes, MK11 3LW, UK
UKHW051830180425
457613UK00022B/1188

9 780367 593063